The Phonological Changes due to the Hamza and Weak Consonant in Arabic

Joyce Åkesson

Pallas Athena

Lund

2010

The Phonological Changes due to the Hamza and Weak Consonant in Arabic

2010 Pallas Athena Distribution, Skarpskyttevägen 10 A, 226 42 Lund, Sweden.

Book design by Joyce Åkesson

ISBN: 978-91-977641-9-3

PRINTED IN THE UNITED STATES OF AMERICA

ALSO BY JOYCE ÅKESSON

Majnūn Leyla: Poems about Passion, Pallas Athena Distribution, December 2009.

The Invitation, Pallas Athena Distribution, July 2009.

Love's Thrilling Dimensions, Pallas Athena Distribution, February 2009.

A Study of the Assimilation and Substitution in Arabic, Pallas Athena Distribution, March 2010.

The Essentials of the Class of the Strong Verb in Arabic, Pallas Athena Distribution, January 2010

The Complexity of the Irregular Verbal and Nominal Forms & the Phonological Changes in Arabic, Pallas Athena Distribution, April 2009.

Arabic Morphology and Phonology: Based on the Marāḥ al-Arwāḥ by Aḥmad b. ᶜAlī b. Masᶜūd, Studies in Semitic Languages and Linguistics, Brill Academic Publishers, July 2001.

Aḥmad B. ᶜAlī B. Masᶜūd on Arabic Morphology, Marāḥ al-Arwāḥ: Part 1: The Strong Verb, Studia Orientalia Lundensia, Vol. 4, Brill Academic Publishers, October 1990.

CONTENTS

2. THE CHANGES DUE TO THE WEAK CONSONANT 45

PREFACE

This work offers a comprehensive overview of the phonological changes due to the hamza and to the weak consonant.

For this purpose it focuses specifically on the complexities of many words pertaining to the classes of the hamzated and weak verbs. In many of these cases, the hamza or weak consonant can be alleviated or retained. Other phonological particularities can also affect the words' structures.

The extensive data, the techniques of the phonological analysis and the references to the different works from the 8th century until our days, offer a thorough and accessible study of both these linguistic phenomena for both the students and researchers of Arabic.

1. THE CHANGES DUE TO THE HAMZA

1.1. The hamza. Its retaining or alleviation

The hamza, which is characterized as the glottal stop, can either be pronounced fully, and is thus transcribed as ʾ, or be alleviated. The reason of its alleviation is that it is a hard heavy consonant uttered from the farthest part of the throat.

There exist some specific rules which determine how the hamza is represented, whether it is maintained or not and which are the changes that are carried out in the word.

As it shal be remarked in this study, these rules depend to a great extent on the hamza's position in a word, on whether it is the inial (cf. 1.1.1.), middle (cf. 1.1.2.) or last segment (cf. 1.1.3.) in it.

A- The "purely" hamzated verb

The hamza is mostly found in the hamzated verb and its derivatives. Thus *al-mahmūz* is the designation given to the verb with a hamza radical.

The hamzated verb falls into three classes that refer to the position of the hamza in their forms:

1- verbs with hamza as their 1st radical, e.g. *ʾaḫaḏa* "to take", *ʾakala* "to eat".

2- verbs with hamza as their 2nd radical, e.g. *saʾala* "to ask", *raʾā* "to see".

3- verbs with hamza as their 3rd radical, e.g. *qaraʾa* "to read", *ǧāʾa* "to come".

1- The conjugation of the verb with 1st radical hamza:

1- *faʿala yafʿulu,* e.g. *ʾaḫaḏa yaʾḫuḏu* "to take".

2- *faʿala yafʿilu,* e.g. *ʾadaba yaʾdibu* "to invite (to a party or banquet)".

3- *faʿala yafʿalu,* e.g. *ʾahaba yaʾhabu* "to prepare".

4- *faʿila yafʿalu,* e.g. *ʾariqa yaʾraqu* "to find no sleep".

5- *faᶜila yafᶜulu,* e.g. *ᵓariǧa yaᵓruǧu* "to be flagrant".

6- *faᶜala yafᶜulu,* e.g. *ᵓasala yaᵓsulu* "to sharpen".

The example *ᵓaḫaḏa* becomes *yaᵓḫuḏu* in the imperfect of the indicative active. Its imperative is *ḫuḏ,* its active participle is *ᵓāḫiḏun,* its *maṣdar* is *ᵓaḫḏun,* its perfect passive is *ᵓuḫiḏa,* its imperfect is *yuᵓḫaḏu* and its passive participle is *maᵓḫūḏun.*

<u>*2- The conjugation of the verb with 2nd radical hamza:*</u>

1- *faᶜala yafᶜalu,* e.g. *saᵓala yasᵓalu* "to ask". The fatḥa is given to its 2nd radical hamza because the hamza is a guttural consonant in the same manner as it is given to the 2nd radical of the strong verb of which the 2nd or 3rd radical is a guttural consonant (cf. par. 3.1.).

2- *faᶜila yafᶜalu,* e.g. *yaᵓisa yayᵓasu* "to despair".

3- *faᶜula yafᶜulu,* e.g. *laᵓuma yalᵓumu* "to be wicked".

The example *saᵓala* "to ask" becomes *yasᵓalu* in the imperfect of the indicative active. Its imperative is *ᵓisᵓal,* its active participle is *sāᵓilun,* its *maṣdar* is *suᵓālun,* its perfect passive is *suᵓila,* its imperfect is *yusᵓalu* and its passive participle is *masᵓūlun.*

3- The conjugation of the verb with 3rd radical hamza:

The verb with 3rd radical hamza falls into the following conjugations:

1- *faᶜala yafᶜulu,* e.g. *sāʾa yasūʾu* "to become evil".

2- *faᶜala yafᶜilu,* e.g. *ǧāʾa yaǧīʾu* "to come", and *hanaʾa yahniʾu* "to be beneficial".

3- *faᶜala yafᶜalu,* e.g. *našaʾa yanšaʾu* "to emerge", and *sabaʾa yasbaʾu.*

4- *faᶜila yafᶜalu,* e.g. *ṣadiʾa yaṣdaʾu* "to become rusty".

5- *faᶜula yafᶜulu,* e.g. *ǧaruʾa yaǧruʾu* "to dare, venture".

The example *qaraʾa* "to read". It becomes *yaqraʾu* in the imperfect of the indicative active. Its imperative is *ʾiqraʾ,* its active participle is *qāriʾun,* its *maṣdar* is *qirāʾatun,* its perfect passive is *quriʾa,* its imperfect is *yuqraʾu* and its passive participle is *maqrūʾun.*

B- The hamzated verb combined with another irregular verb

The hamza can occur as a radical in other classes of verbs than the "purely" hamzated. The following cases can be mentioned:

1- as a 1st radical in the doubled verb, e.g. *ʾanna yaʾinnu* "to groan, moan".

2- as a 2nd radical in verbs with weak 1st radical, e.g. *waʾada* "to bury alive (a newborn girl)", and as a 3rd radical in a verb with weak 1st radical, e.g. *wağaʾa* "to beat".

3- as a 1st or 3rd radical in verbs with weak 2nd radical, e.g. *ʾāna* "to come, to approach" and *ğāʾa* "to come" respectively.

4- as a 1st or 2nd radical in verbs with weak 3rd radical, e.g. *ʾabā* [with final *alif maqṣūra]* "to refuse" and *raʾā* [with final *alif maqṣūra]* "to see" respectively.

5- as a 2nd radical in verbs with weak 1st and 3rd radical, e.g. *waʾā* [with final *alif maqṣūra]* "to promise".

6- as a 1st radical in verbs with 2nd and 3rd weak radical, e.g. *ʾawā* [with final *alif maqṣūra]* "to seek refuge".

1.1.1. The hamza as the initial segment of a word

The hamza that occurs as the initial segment of a word is written over the alif when it is vowelled by a fatḥa, e.g. *ʾabun* "father" (أَبٌ) or by a ḍamma, e.g. *ʾummun* "mother" (أُمٌّ), and under the alif when it vowelled by a kasra, e.g. *ʾismun* "name" (إِسمٌ).

The alleviation of the hamza is regular when it concerns the connective hamza following a vowel in the word preceding it, as it becomes a *waṣla* (for discussions see Wright, I, 19-20). An example is the hamza vowelled by a fatḥa, *ʾa,* of the definite article -*ʾal* that becomes -*l* after the alleviation with the *waṣla,* e.g. *bintu l-rāʿī* (بِنْتُ ٱلرَّاعِي) said instead of *bintu ʾal-rāʿī* (بِنْتُ أَلرَّاعِي) "the shepherd's daughter".

The alleviation of the hamza can be considered as anomalous in other cases. Some anomalous examples are *ʾunāsun* that becomes *nāsun* "people" after the elision of the hamza (cf. Ibn Ğinnī, *Ḫaṣāʾiṣ III,* 151, Ibn Manẓūr, I, 147, Howell, I, fasc. I, 174, Fleisch, *Traité I,* 151) and *al-ʾilāhu* that becomes *al-lāhu* after the elision of the hamza (cf. Åkesson, *Ibn Masʿūd* 242-243: fol. 23a, Ibn Manẓūr, I, 114).

1.1.2. The hamza preceded by another segment in the middle of the word

The hamza can be found in other positions than as the initial segment of a word. In this case it is found in a sequence in which it is preceded by another segment. This segment can be a consonant which is another consonant than the hamza, another hamza or a glide, and it can be vowelled or vowelless.

Furthermore, as it shall be remarked in some cases, the sequence can occur in one word or in two words following each other. For a better understanding of the retaining of the hamza or the changes which can affect it, the sequences are introduced in two categories. In one of them, the segment preceding the hamza is a consonant or a glide, and in the other one, the segment is a hamza.

1.1.2.1. The hamza is vowelless and the segment preceding it is vowelled: its retaining or the alleviation by the change of the hamza into a glide.

1.1.2.2. The hamza and the segment preceding it are vowelled.

1.1.2.2.1. The hamza is vowelled by one of the three vowels and is preceded by a fatḥa: its alleviation by its change into a *hamza bayna bayna* "an intermediary hamza".

1.1.2.2.2. The hamza is vowelled by a fatḥa and is preceded by a ḍamma or kasra: its alleviation by its change into a glide.

1.1.2.3. The hamza is vowelled and the segment preceding it is vowelless.

1.1.2.3.1. The hamza is vowelled by a fatḥa and is preceded by a sukūn: its elision together with the hamza's fatḥa shifted to the vowelless segment preceding it.

1.1.2.3.2. The hamza is vowelled by a fatḥa and is preceded by a sukūn [i.e. a vowelless infixed glide of prolongation]: its assimilation to the glide.

1.1.2.3.3. The hamza is vowelled by a kasra and is preceded by a sukūn [i.e. a vowelless infixed glide of prolongation]: its assimilation to the glide.

1.1.2.3.1. The hamza is vowelled by a kasra or ḍamma and is preceded by a sukūn [i.e. a vowelless infixed glide of prolongation]: its change into a *hamza bayna bayna.*

With regards to the fact that the segment preceding the hamza can be another hamza, the following sequences are presented:

1.1.2.4. The hamza is vowelless and the hamza preceding it is vowelled by a fatḥa: its alleviation by its change into an *ā*.

1.1.2.5. The hamza is vowelless and the hamza preceding it is vowelled by a kasra: its alleviation by its change into a *y*.

1.1.2.6. The hamza is vowelless and the hamza preceding it is vowelled by a ḍamma: its change into a *w* or its elision.

1.1.2.7. The hamza and the hamza preceding it are vowelled by a fatḥa.

1.1.2.7.1. The hamza and the hamza preceding it are vowelled by a fatḥa in one word: their assimilation into a *madda* and the anomalous insertion of an *ā* in some cases.

1.1.2.7.2. The hamza is vowelled by a fatḥa in one word and follows a hamza vowelled by a fatḥa in the word preceding it: the elision of one hamza or of both.

It shall be remarked in this study that the alleviation of the hamza is carried out by changing it either into a glide or a *hamza bayna bayna* "an intermediary hamza" or by eliding it.

1.1.2.1. The hamza is vowelless and the segment preceding it is vowelled: its retaining or the alleviation by the change of the hamza into a glide:

The hamza can be found in a sequence in which it occurs vowelless and the segment preceding it can be vowelled by a fatḥa, a ḍamma or a kasra. In all these three cases the hamza can be maintained or alleviated. In the latter case, it is changed into a glide of the same nature of the vowel of the segment preceding it (cf. Åkesson, *Ibn Masᶜūd* 240: fol. 21b, Roman, *Étude I,* 330).

When the hamza is maintained, it is the vowel of the segment preceding it that determines its shape. If the hamza is preceded by a ḍamma it is changed into a *w* with a hamza over it, e.g. *luʾmun* "blame" (لُؤْمٌ) written with a hamza over the *w* instead of *luʾmun* written with the hamza over the alif, and when it is preceded by the kasra it is changed into a *hamza ᶜalā kursī l-yāʾ*, e.g. *biʾrun* "well, spring" written with the *hamza ᶜalā kursī l-yāʾ* (بِئْرٌ) instead of *biʾrun* written with the hamza under the alif (cf. Wright, II, 72).

In other cases when the hamza is alleviated, it is noted that the vowel of the segment preceding it determines the nature of the glide that the hamza is changed into. If this vowel is a fatḥa the hamza is changed into an *ā* (cf. 1.1.2.1.: 1., 1.1.2.4.), if it is a ḍamma it is changed into an *ū* (cf. 1.1.2.1.: 2., 1.1.2.6.) and if it is a kasra it is changed into an *ī* (cf. 1.1.2.1.: 3., 1.1.2.5.).

1- The alleviation by the change of the vowelless hamza, the ʾ, into an ā:

If the segment preceding the hamza is vowelled by a fatḥa the hamza is changed into an *ā*. Thus:

-aʾ ➠ *-(a)ā*

An example is *raʾsun* with the vowelless ʾ preceded by a fatḥa that becomes *r(a)āsun* "a head" after the change of the ʾ into *ā*.

<u>*2- The alleviation by the change of the vowelless hamza, the ʾ, into an ū:*</u>

If the segment preceding the hamza is vowelled by a ḍamma the hamza is changed into an *ū*. Thus:

-uʾ ➠ *-(u)ū*

An example is *luʾmun* with the vowelless ʾ preceded by a ḍamma that becomes *l(u)ūmun* "blame" after the change of the ʾ into *ū*.

<u>*3- The alleviation by the change of the vowelless hamza, the ʾ, into an ī:*</u>

If the segment preceding the hamza is vowelled by a kasra the hamza is changed into an *ī*. Thus:

-iʾ ➠ *-(i)ī*

An example is *biʾrun* with the vowelless ʾ preceded by a kasra that becomes *b(i)īrun* "well, spring" after the change of the ʾ into *ī*.

1.1.2.2. The hamza and the segment preceding it are vowelled:

The vowelled state of both the hamza and the segment preceding it give rise to the following eventualities:

1.1.2.2.1. The hamza is vowelled by one of the three vowels and is preceded by a fatḥa: its retaining or its alleviation by its change into a *hamza bayna bayna* "an intermediary hamza".

1.1.2.2.2. The hamza is vowelled by a fatḥa and is preceded by a ḍamma or kasra: its alleviation by its change into a glide.

1.1.2.2.1. The hamza is vowelled by one of the three vowels and is preceded by a fatḥa: its retaining or its alleviation by its change into a hamza bayna bayna "an intermediary hamza":

The hamza that is vowelled by one of the three vowels and preceded by a fatḥa can be changed into a *hamza bayna bayna* "intermediary hamza" (for discussions concerning it see

Sībawaihi, II, 168-169, Åkesson, *Ibn Mas^cūd* 240: 21b, Roman, 324-326, Lane, I, 288).

When the hamza that is vowelled by a ḍamma or a kasra is maintained, it is represented by its being written over - in the case of the *ᵓu,* or under, - in the case of the *ᵓi,* the particular glide that its vowel is connected to (for discussions see de Sacy, I, 95, Wright, II, 75). If the hamza is vowelled by a ḍamma that is underlyingly written over an alif, the *ᵓu,* it is changed into a hamza over the *w*. An example is *laᵓuma* "to be wicked" (لَؤُم) written with the hamza over the *w* instead of the base form *laᵓuma* (لأُم) written with a hamza over the alif vowelled by a ḍamma. If the hamza is vowelled by a kasra that is underlyingly written under the alif, the *ᵓi,* it is changed into a *hamza ᶜalā kursī l-yāᵓ*. An example is *saᵓima* "to be weary" (سَئِم) written with the *hamza ᶜalā kursī l-yāᵓ* instead of the base form *saᵓima* (سَإِم) written with a hamza under the alif.

A closer look at the alleviated hamza will make one remark that it is a sort of mixture between the hamza itself and the glide to which its vowel is connected to. If the hamza's vowel is a fatḥa, then the glide that it is connected to is the *ā,* e.g. *s(a)āla* from *saᵓala* "to ask" (cf. 1.1.2.2.1.: 1), if it is a ḍamma then the glide that it is connected to is a *w,* e.g. *lawuma* from *laᵓuma* "he was base" (cf. 1.1.2.2.1.: 2), and if it is a kasra then the glide that it is connected to is a *y*, e.g. *sayima* from *saʾima* "he was weary" (cf. 1.1.2.2.1.: 3).

Concerning the alleviated hamza Ibn Ǧinnī, *Sirr I*, 48 writes:

> "As what concerns the alleviated hamza it is the one that is termed *hamza bayna bayna*. The meaning with Sībawaihi's saying of *bayna bayna* is that it is intermediary between the hamza and the segment to which its vowel is connected to. If it is vowelled by the fatḥa it is then between the hamza and the alif, if it is vowelled by the kasra it is then between the hamza and the *y*, and if it is vowelled by the ḍamma it is then between the hamza and the *w*... As what concerns the one vowelled by the fatḥa it is in your saying about *saʾala* "he asked": *sāla*, as what concerns the one vowelled by the kasra it is in your saying about *saʾima* "he was weary": *sayima*, and as what concerns the one vowelled by the ḍamma it is in your saying concerning *laʾuma* "he was base": *lawuma*".

Nöldeke, *Grammatik* 5 compares the *hamza bayna bayna* with the french diphthong *oi, ie* or the Dutch *ooi, eeu,* etc. This hamza is considered as vowelless according to the Kufans whereas it is provided by a faint vowel close to the sukūn according to the Basrans (for their debate see Ibn al-Anbārī, *Inṣāf* Q. 105, 306-307). A curiosity worth to be mentioned is that the expression *bayna bayna* has been used in a line said by the poet Abū Nuwās, *Dīwān* 588 (cf. Monteil, *Abū Nuwās* 36) who refers to someone *bayna bayna* "in between [a male and a female]", i.e. the so-called effeminate boy. It is Ibn Ǧinnī, *Sirr I,* 49 who remarks having heard this expression from Abū ᶜAlī, who cites Abu Nuwās's verses:

"Wa-ḫuḏ min kaffi ǧāriyatin waṣīfin
malīḥi l-dalli malṯūġi l-kalāmi
lahu šaklu l-ʾināṯi wa-bayna baynin
tarā fīhi takādiyata l-ġulāmi".
"And take [the drink] from the hand of a beautiful
flirting cupbearer, lisping in 'her' speech.
He has the figure of a female and of someone 'in
between [a male and a female]'.
You remark on him the boy's parting of the hair".

1- The alleviation by the change of the hamza vowelled by a fatha, the ʾa, into an ā:

If the hamza is vowelled by a fatḥa and is preceded by one it can be changed into an *ā*. Thus:

-aʾa ➠ *-(a)ā*

An example is *saʾala* "to ask" with the hamza vowelled by a fatḥa, the *ʾa*, preceded by a fatḥa, that becomes *s(a)āla*.

An example concerning the hamza alleviated for the sake of metric exigency, is the verb with 3rd radical hamza *hanaʾaki* that is said *han(a)āki* (cf. Åkesson, *Ibn Masʿūd* 240: fol. 22a) in a verse composed by Farazdaq, which is cited by Sībawaihi, II, 175, Ibn Ǧinnī, *Ḫaṣāʾiṣ III,* 152, *Sirr II,* 666, Ibn al-Sarrāǧ, *Uṣūl III,* 469, Muʾaddib, *Taṣrīf* 530, Zamaḫšarī, 166, Ibn Yaʿīš, IX, 113, *Mulūkī* 229, Ibn ʿUṣfūr, I, 405, Howell, IV, fasc. I, 951, Åkesson, *Ibn Masʿūd* 255: (220). It runs as follows:

> *"Rāḥat bi-Maslamata l-biġālu ʿašīyata*
> *fa-rʿā Fazāratu lā hanāki l-martaʿu"*
> "The mules have gone away with Maslama at
> evening.
> Then graze your camels, Fazāra. May the pasture
> not be pleasant to you!".

2- The alleviation by the change of the hamza vowelled by a ḍamma, the ʾu, into wu:

If the hamza is vowelled by a ḍamma and is preceded by a fatḥa, it can be changed into a *w*. Thus:

-aʾu ➠ *-awu*

An example is *la*ˀ*uma* "to be base" with the hamza vowelled by a ḍamma: ˀ*u,* and preceded by a fatḥa, that becomes *lawuma* with the change of the ˀ*u* into *wu.*

3- The alleviation by the change of the hamza vowelled by a kasra the ˀ*i, into yi:*

If the hamza is vowelled by a kasra and is preceded by a fatḥa, it can be changed into a y vowelled by a kasra.

*-a*ˀ*i* ➠ *-ayi*

An example is *sa*ˀ*ima* "he was weary" with the hamza vowelled by a kasra: ˀ*i,* preceded by a fatḥa that becomes *sayima* with the change of the ˀ*i* into *yi.*

1.1.2.2.2. The hamza is vowelled by a fatḥa and is preceded by a ḍamma or kasra: its alleviation by its change into a glide:

If the hamza is vowelled by a fatḥa and is preceded by a ḍamma or a kasra, it is changed into a glide of the same nature of the vowel of the segment preceding it (cf. Åkesson, *Ibn Mas*ᶜ*ūd* 240: fol. 21b). If the vowel preceding it is a ḍamma, then the hamza is changed into an *w* (cf. 1.1.2.2.2.: 1) and if it is a kasra it is changed into a *y* (cf. 1.1.2.2.2.: 2).

1- The change of the hamza preceded by a ḍamma into w:

If the segment preceding the hamza is a ḍamma, the hamza can be changed into a *w*. Thus:

-uʾa ➠ *-uwa*

An example is *guʾanun* "receptable for bottles or the like" with the hamza vowelled by a fatḥa preceded by a ḍamma that becomes *ǧuwanun* with the change of the ʾ into a *w* (cf. Zamaḫšarī, 174, Ibn Ǧinnī, *Sirr II,* 573, Åkesson, *Ibn Masʿūd* 240: 21b).

2- The change of the hamza preceded by a kasra into y:

If the segment preceding the hamza is a kasra, the hamza can be changed into a *y*. Thus:

-iʾa ➠ *-iya*

An example is *miʾarun* "exciting dissension among the people" with the hamza vowelled by a fatḥa preceded by a kasra that becomes *miyarun* with the change of the ʾ into a *y* (cf. Sībawaihi, II, 169, Zamaḫšarī, 166, Åkesson, *Ibn Masʿūd* 240: fol. 21b).

It can be observed that the hamza that is vowelled by a fatḥa and preceded by a ḍamma or kasra, is changed in the same manner as the hamza that is vowelless and preceded by a vowel (for it see par. 1.1.2.1.), i.e. into a glide of the nature of the specific vowel preceding it.

1.1.2.3. The hamza is vowelled and the segment preceding it is vowelless:

The vowelled state of the hamza and the vowelless state of the segment preceding it give rise to the following eventualities:

1.1.2.3.1. The hamza is vowelled by a fatḥa and is preceded by a sukūn: its elision together with the hamza's fatḥa shifted to the vowelless segment preceding it.

1.1.2.3.2. The hamza is vowelled by a fatḥa and is preceded by a sukūn [i.e. a vowelless infixed glide of prolongation]: its assimilation to the glide.

1.1.2.3.3. The hamza is vowelled by a kasra and is preceded by a sukūn [i.e. a vowelless infixed glide of prolongation]: its assimilation to the glide.

1.1.2.3.4. The hamza is vowelled by a kasra or ḍamma and is preceded by a sukūn [i.e. a vowelless infixed glide of prolongation]: its change into a *hamza bayna bayna.*

1.1.2.3.1. The hamza is vowelled by a fatḥa and is preceded by a sukūn: its elision together with the hamza's fatḥa shifted to the vowelless segment preceding it:

If the hamza is vowelled by a fatḥa and is preceded by a vowelless segment, it can be elided and its fatḥa is shifted to the segment preceding it (cf. Åkesson, *Ibn Mas*^{c}*ūd* 240-242: fols. 22a-22b)

The vowelless segment preceding the hamza can be:

1- a strong segment.

2- an original *w* or *y*.

3- an augmentative *w* or *y* attached to the pattern.

1.1.2.3.1.1. The vowelless segment preceding the hamza is a strong segment:

The strong vowelless segment preceding the hamza vowelled by a fatḥa can be the *l-* of the definite article, *al-,* or a radical. The change procedure is that the hamza's fatḥa is shifted to the vowelless strong segment and the hamza is elided.

An example in which the segment preceding the hamza is the vowelless *l-* of the definite article is *al-ʾaḥmaru* "red" with the *l-* of the definite article, *al-,* vowelless preceding the hamza vowelled by a fatḥa. This sequence leads to the elision of the hamza and the transfer of its fatḥa to the *l* preceding it, namely *ʾalaḥmaru.* Another variant exists as well, namely *laḥmaru* with the hamza of the article elided (cf. Sībawaihi, II, 170, Zamaḫšarī, 166-167, Åkesson, *Ibn Masʿūd* 240: fol. 22a, Howell, IV, fasc. I, 942-943, 959-963, Lane, I, 74, Wright, II, 269).

Some examples in which the segment preceding the hamza is a radical is the imperfect with the 2nd radical hamza *yasʾalu* "he asks" that becomes anomalously *yasalu* (cf. de Sacy, I, 236, Wright, II, 77, Vernier, I, 74), and *yarʾ(a)ā* "he sees" that becomes *yar(a)ā* (cf. Sībawaihi, II, 170) on account of the frequency of its usage (cf. Åkesson, *Ibn Masʿūd* 244: fol. 23a-23b). It can be remarked that in both *yasʾalu* and *yarʾ(a)ā,* the ʾ

is elided and the hamza's fatḥa is shifted to the vowelless segment preceding it.

Concerning *yarʾā,* it can be mentioned that in poetry, in consideration to the metric exigency, the ʾ can be retained. This is remarked in *tarʾayāhu* that is used instead of *tarayāhu* in this verse said by Surāqa b. Mirdās al-Azdī al-Bāriqī cited by Ibn Ǧinnī *Sirr I,* 77, II, 826, *Ḫaṣāʾiṣ III,* 153, *de Flexione* 34, Muʾaddib, *Taṣrīf* 422, Ibn Yaᶜīš, *Mulūkī* 370, Ibn Manẓūr, III, 1538, Ibn ᶜUṣfūr, II, 621, Howell, IV, fasc. I, 941, Åkesson, *Ibn Masᶜūd* 266: (236):

" ʾUrī ᶜaynayya mā lam tarʾayāhu
kilānā ᶜālimun bi-l-turhāti".
"I make my eyes see what they have not seen:
each of us is knowing in falsehoods".

The elision of the hamza and the transfer of its fatḥa to the vowelless segment preceding it occurs as well in the *maṣdar masʾalatun* "a matter" that becomes *masalatun* (cf. Zamaḫšarī, 166, Åkesson, *Ibn Masᶜūd* 240: fol. 22a).

Another example is *malʾakun* "angel" (from *ʾalaka* "to convey") with the 2nd radical *l* vowelless, preceding the hamza vowelled by a fatḥa. This sequence results in the elision of the hamza and the transfer of its fatḥa to the *l* preceding it, namely *malakun* (cf. Ibn Ğinnī, *Munṣif II*, 102-104, Ibn Manẓūr, I, 110-111, Åkesson, *Ibn Mas*ᶜ*ūd* 240: fol. 22a, Wright, II, 77, Vernier, I, 101-102, Lane, I, 81-82).

1.1.2.3.1.2. The vowelless segment preceding the hamza is a vowelless w or y:

The vowelless *w* or *y* preceding the hamza vowelled by a fatḥa can be an infixed segment or a radical. This sequence results in the elision of the hamza and the transfer of its fatḥa to the segment preceding it. It can be remarked that this sequence can occur in one word or in two words following each other.

1.1.2.3.1.2.1. The elision of the hamza in one word and the transfer of its fatha to the segment preceding it:

The vowelless segment preceding the hamza vowelled by a fatḥa in the same word can be an infixed glide, namely a *w* or a *y*. The conditions of the hamza's elision and consequently of the transfer of its fatḥa to the segment preceding it, is that the infixed segment is not a segment of prolongation, i.e. a glide lengthening the sound of the vowel preceding it, as the *w* in *maf*ᶜ*uwlatun (/ maf*ᶜ*(u)ūlatun)* that lengthens the ḍamma preceding it (for discussions see 1.1.2.3.2.: 1), or the *y* in *faᶜiylatun (/ faᶜ(i)īlatun)* that lengthens the kasra preceding it (for discussions see 1.1.2.3.2. :2) and that the infixed segment is not specific for the diminutive, as the *y* in *ᵓufayᵓilun,* because in these cases the hamza is assimilated to the glide preceding it (for discussions see 1.1.2.3.3.).

1- The segment preceding the hamza is a vowelless w:

If the segment preceding the hamza is a vowelless *w* the procedure is the following:

-wᵓa ➠ *-wa*

An example *is ǧawᵓabatun* "*Ǧawᵓaba* [name of a water]", which is from the root *ǧ ᵓ b* (cf. Howell, IV, fasc. I, 938), in which the infixed *w* is there to make it identical to the pattern *fawᶜalatun.* As it is noticed, the *w* infix is vowelless and precedes the hamza vowelled by a fatḥa. This sequence results in the elision of the hamza and the transfer of its fatḥa to the *w* preceding it, namely *ǧawabatun* (cf. Åkesson, *Ibn Masᶜūd* 240: fol. 22a).

2- The segment preceding the hamza is a vowelless y:

If the segment preceding the hamza is a vowelless *y* the procedure is the following:

-yʾa ➠ *-ya*

An example is *ǧayʾalun* "female hyena", which is from the root *ǧ ʾ l* (cf. Ibn Manẓūr, I, 529, Lane, I, 370), in which the infixed *y* is there to make it identical to the pattern *fayᶜalun.* As it is remarked, the *y* infix is vowelless and precedes the hamza vowelled by a fatḥa. This sequence results in the elision of the hamza and the transfer of its fatḥa to the *y* preceding it, namely *ǧayalun* (cf. Åkesson, *Ibn Masᶜūd* 240: fol. 22a).

1.1.2.3.1.2.2. The elision of the hamza vowelled by a fatḥa in one word following a vowelless w, y or a strong segment in the word preceding it and the transfer of its fatḥa to this segment:

The elision of the hamza that is vowelled by a fatḥa is as well carried out if the vowelless *w, y* or the strong segment preceding it, is not in the same word as the hamza. In this case the vowelled hamza, which is the initial segment of the second word, is elided, and its vowel, the fatḥa, is shifted to the vowelless segment preceding it which is the ultimate segment of the word preceding it (for a study see Sībawaihi, II, 171-172, Zamaḫšarī, 166, Åkesson, *Ibn Mas*ᶜ*ūd* 240-242: fol. 22a, Howell, IV, fasc. I, 938 sqq., Vernier, I, 104).

1- The segment preceding the hamza in the word preceding it is a vowelless w:

If the vowelless weak ultimate segment in the word preceding the hamza vowelled by a fatḥa is a *w,* the procedure is the following:

-*w* + ᵓ*a* ➠ -*wa*

An example is *ᵓAbuw ᵓAyyūba* "the father of Job", with the *w* vowelless in *ᵓAbuw (ᵓAb(u)ū),* marking its nominative's ending as it is the 1st element of the construct state, which precedes the hamza vowelled by a fatḥa that is the initial segment of the second word. This sequence results in the elision of the hamza from *ᵓAyyūba* and the transfer of its fatḥa to the *w* preceding it, namely *ᵓAbuwa yyūba* (cf. Åkesson, *Ibn Mas*ᶜ*ūd* 240-242: fol. 22a, Howell, IV, fasc. I, 940).

Some other examples with the alleviation of the hamza, just to mention a few, are *ḏuw ᵓamrihim* "the author of their matter" which becomes *ḏuwa mrihim* (Ibn Yaᶜīš, IX, 109) and *qāḍuw ᵓabīka* "the judges of your father" which becomes *qāḍuwa bīka* (cf. Ibn Yaᶜīš, IX, 110, Howell, IV, fasc. I, 940).

2- *The segment preceding the hamza in the word preceding it is a vowelless y:*

If the vowelless weak ultimate segment in the word preceding the hamza vowelled by a fatḥa is a *y,* the procedure is the following:

-y + *ᵓa* ➠ *-ya*

An example is *ᵓabtaġiy ᵓamrahu* "I seek for his matter" with the *y* vowelless occuring as the 3rd radical of the first word *ᵓabtaġiy,* - which is the imperfect of 1st person of the sing. of *baġiya* -, preceding the hamza vowelled by a fatḥa that is the first initial segment of the second word, *ᵓamrahu.* This sequence results in the elision of the hamza from *ᵓamrahu* and the transfer of its fatḥa to the *y* preceding it, namely *ᵓabtaġiya mrahu* (cf. Åkesson, *Ibn Masᶜūd* 240-242: fol. 22a, Howell, IV, fasc. I, 940).

3- The segment preceding the hamza in the word preceding it is a vowelless strong segment:

If the vowelless ultimate segment in the word preceding the hamza vowelled by a fatḥa is a strong segment, the procedure is the following [C stands for consonant]:

-C + ʾa ➠ *-Ca*

An example is *man ʾabūka* with the strong segment, the *n,* vowelless occurring as the ultimate segment of the first word, namely the interrogative particle *man,* preceding the hamza vowelled by a fatḥa that is the first initial segment of the second word, *ʾabūka.* This sequence results in the elision of the hamza from *ʾabūka* and the transfer of its fatḥa to the *n* preceding it, namely *mana būka* "who is your father?" (cf. Ibn Yaᶜīš, IX, 110, Howell, IV, fasc. I, 940, Roman, *Étude I,* 332).

Another example is *qad ʾaflaḥa* of the sur. 23: 1 *(qad ʾaflaḥa l-muʾminūna)* "The Believers must (eventually) win through", in which the strong segment, the *d,* of the first word, namely the particle *qad,* is vowelless and precedes the hamza vowelled by a fatḥa that is the initial segment of the second word, namely the verb in the Form IV *ʾaflaḥa.* This sequence results in the alleviation of the hamza from *ʾaflaḥa* in the reading of some, by methods of eliding it and shifting its vowel to the segment preceding it, namely *qada flaḥa l-muʾminūna* (cf. Ibn Yaᶜīš, IX, 110).

Other examples, just to mention a few, are *law ʾanna* that becomes *lawa nna* "if" (with the hamza of *ʾanna* changed into a *waṣla* over the alif) and *qad ʾaṣbaḥa* that becomes *qada ṣbaḥa* "he has become" (with the hamza of ʾaṣbaḥa changed into a *waṣla* over the alif) (cf. Nöldeke, *Grammatik* 5).

1.1.2.3.2. The hamza is vowelled by a fatḥa and is preceded by a sukūn [i.e. a vowelless infixed glide of prolongation]: its assimilation to the glide:

The vowelless segment preceding the hamza vowelled by a fatḥa can be an infixed glide of prolongation. This sequence results in the alleviation of the hamza by its change into the same segment as the segment preceding it, namely a glide, and then the assimilation of the glides. It is worth to have in mind that if the infixed segment is not an infixed glide of prolongation, and the hamza's vowel is a fatḥa, the hamza is elided and its fatḥa is shifted to the segment preceding it (for discussions see par. 1.1.2.3.1.).

Some examples considering two vowelless segments of prolongation in some patterns are the *w* in *mafᶜ(u)wlatun (/*

mafᶜ(u)ūlatun) lengthening the ḍamma preceding it and the *y* in *faᶜ(i)ylatun (/ faᶜ(i)īlatun)* lengthening the kasra preceding it. The cases are discussed below.

1- The segment preceding the hamza is an infixed vowelless w:

If the infixed segment is a vowelless *w* as the *w* in *mafᶜ(u)wlatun (/ mafᶜ(u)ūlatun)* lengthening the ḍamma preceding it, the procedure leading to the assimilation is the following:

-uwʾa ➠ *-uwwa*

An example is *maqruwʾatun (> maqr(u)ūʾatun)* "a writing read" which is formed according to the pattern *mafᶜuwlatun* with the infixed prolonged *w* lengthening the sound of the ḍamma preceding it. The hamza vowelled by a fatḥa is alleviated by its change into the same segment as the segment preceding it, which is a *w*, and then an assimilation of the wāws is carried out resulting in *maqruwwatun* (for discussions see Sībawaihi, II, 171, 175, Åkesson, *Ibn Masᶜūd* 242: fols. 22a-22b, Howell, IV, fasc. I, 936-937, de Sacy, I, 370, Vernier, I, 102, 350).

2- The segment preceding the hamza is an infixed vowelless y:

If the infixed segment is a vowelless *y* as the *y* in *faᶜiylatun (/ faᶜ(i)īlatun)* lengthening the kasra preceding it, the procedure leading to the assimilation is the following:

-iyᵓa ➠ *-iyya*

An example is *ḫaṭiyᵓatun (> ḫaṭ(i)īᵓatun)* "an error, sin", which is formed according to the pattern *faᶜiylatun* with the infixed *y* lengthening the sound of the kasra preceding it. The hamza vowelled by a fatḥa is alleviated by its change into the same segment as the segment preceding it, namely a *y*, and then an assimilation of the yāᵓs is carried out resulting in *ḫaṭ(i)yyatun* (for discussions see Sībawaihi, II, 171, 175, Åkesson, *Ibn Masᶜūd* 242: fol. 22a-22b, Howell, IV, fasc. I, 936-937, de Sacy, I, 370, Vernier, I, 102, 350).

1.1.2.3.3. The hamza is vowelled by a kasra and is preceded by a sukūn [i.e. a vowelless infixed glide of prolongation]: its assimilation to the glide:

A pattern in which the hamza vowelled by a kasra is preceded by an infixed vowelless *y* is *ᵓufayᶜilun,* in which the *y* is specific for the diminutive. The procedure leading to the assimilation is the following:

*-ay*ʾ*i* ➠ *-ayyi*

An example is *ʾufayʾisun* "a kind of little hoe, a little axe", which is formed according to the pattern *ʾufayʾilun* with the vowelless infixed *y* specific for the diminutive. The hamza vowelled by a kasra is alleviated by its change into the same segment as the segment preceding it, namely a *y,* and then an assimilation of the yāʾs is carried out resulting in *ʾufayyisun* (for discussions see Sībawaihi, II, 171, 175, Åkesson, *Ibn Masʿūd* 242: fol. 22a-22b, Howell, IV, fasc. I, 936-937, de Sacy, I, 370, Vernier, I, 102, 350).

1.1.2.3.4. The hamza is vowelled by a kasra or damma and is preceded by a sukūn [i.e. a vowelless infixed glide of prolongation]: its change into a hamza bayna bayna:

As examples of two patterns in which the hamza vowelled by a kasra is preceded by an infixed vowelless *ā* of prolongation, the active participle *f(a)āʿilun* and the broken pl. of the nouns *maf(a)āʿilun* in which the alif lengthens the sound of the fatḥa preceding it, can be taken up. This sequence results in the alleviation of the hamza by its change into a *hamza bayna bayna* (for discussions see Sībawaihi, II, 171, Roman, *Étude I,* 333). The procedure leading to the assimilation is the following:

- (a)āʾi ➠ *-(a)āyi*

Some examples that are formed according to the active participle *f(a)āᶜilun* are *s(a)āʾilun* "a questioner" with the 2nd radical hamza vowelled by a kasra, from *saʾala* "to ask", which results after the change of the hamza into a *hamza bayna bayna* in *s(a)āyilun,* and *q(a)āʾilun* "a teller" from *q(a)āwilun* with the 2nd radical *w* changed into a hamza vowelled by a kasra, from *qawala* "to tell", which results after the change in *q(a)āyilun* (cf. Åkesson, *Ibn Masᶜūd* 242: fol. 22b).

An example that is formed according to the broken pl. of the nouns *maf(a)āᶜilun* is *mas(a)āʾilun* "questions" (cf. Sībawaihi, II, 171, Roman, *Étude I*, 333) which results in *mas(a)āyilun.*

If the hamza is vowelled by a ḍamma an preceded by an *ā* of prolongation, the procedure leading to the assimilation is the following:

-āʾu ➠ *-āwu*

An example in which the hamza vowelled by a ḍamma is preceded by an *ā* of prolongation is *ǧazā(a)ʾun* "a recompense" that is formed according to the pattern *faᶜ(a)ālun* in which the alif lengthens the sound of the fatḥa preceding it. It occurs in the sentence presented by Sībawaihi, II, 171 *ǧazāʾu ʾummihi* "his mother's recompense" (جَزاءُ أمّه) This hamza is changed into a *hamza bayna bayna* resulting in *ǧazāwu mmihi* (جَزاوُامّه) (cf. ibid, Roman, *Étude I,* 333).

1.1.2.4. The hamza is vowelless and the hamza preceding it is vowelled by a fatha: Its alleviation by its change into an ā:

The hamza that is vowelless and preceded by a hamza vowelled by a fatḥa at the initial of the word is changed into an *ā,* and hence the hamza is assimilated to the *ā* resulting in a madda.

The procedure is the following:

-ʾaʾ ➠ *-ʾ(a)ā*

Some examples that can be mentioned are those formed according to the pattern *ʾafᶜalu,* e.g. *ʾaʾḫaḏu* "the one who holds mostly against" that becomes *ʾ(a)āḫaḏu* and *ʾaʾdamu* "tawny, dark-complexioned" that becomes *ʾ(a)ādamu* with the *madda* as their initial segment (cf. Sībawaihi, II, 174, Ibn Ǧinnī, *Sirr II,* 579, 665, Åkesson, *Ibn Masᶜūd* 242: fol. 22b).

1.1.2.4.1. An anomalous example: *ᵓayimmatun*

An anomalous example in which both hamzas are maintained is the base form of the plural of *ᵓimām,* namely *ᵓaᵓmimatun* in which this combination of the hamzas takes place at the initial of the word. The 2nd hamza is changed into *y* for the purpose of alleviation and the kasra of the *m* is shifted to it, namely *ᵓayimmatun* (cf. Zamaḫšarī, 167, Ibn Manẓūr, I, 133, Howell, IV, fasc. I 971 sqq., Lane, I, 91, Vernier, I, 101), because the combination of two hamzas at the initial of the word is deemed as heavy. The Kufans however maintain both the hamzas anomalously as they recite the sur. 9: 12 as *(fa-qātilū ᵓaᵓimmata l-kufri)* "Fight ye the chiefs of Unfaith", with *ᵓaᵓimmata* read instead of *ᵓayimmata* (cf. Ibn Ḫālawaihi, *Qirāᵓāt I,* 235, Åkesson, *Ibn Masᶜūd* 242: fol. 22b). This reading is disliked by Ibn Ǧinnī (cf. Ibn Ǧinnī, *Ḫaṣāᵓiṣ III,* 143, *Sirr I,* 81).

It can be remarked that the combination of both hamzas at the interior of the word is more permitted. An example is *ḫaṭāᵓiᵓī* "my sins" used instead of *ḫaṭāyāya* in the sentence *ᵓallahumma ġfir lī ḫaṭāᵓiī* "O God forgive me my sins", which according to Zamaḫšarī, 167, Abū Zaid has heard from Abū l-Samḥ and his cousin Raddād.

1.1.2.5. The hamza is vowelless and the hamza preceding it is vowelled by a kasra: its alleviation by its change into a y:

The hamza that is vowelless and preceded by a hamza vowelled by a kasra is changed into a *y*.

The procedure is the following:

-*ʾiʾ* ➠ -*ʾ(i)y*

An example in which such a combination occurs is the imperative of the 2nd person of the masc. sing. of a verb with 1st hamza radical *ʾasara* "to capture", namely *ʾiʾsir* "capture!" with the 2nd vowelless hamza preceded by a kasra which becomes *ʾ(i)ysir* with the *ʾ* changed into a *y*, and as the vowelless *y* in it is preceded by a kasra, it becomes *ʾ(i)īsir* with the *y* assimilated to the kasra resulting in the lengthened *ī* (cf. Åkesson, *Ibn Masʿūd* 242: fol. 22b).

1.1.2.6. The hamza is vowelless and the hamza preceding it is vowelled by a ḍamma: its change into a w or its elision:

The hamza that is vowelless and preceded by a hamza vowelled by a ḍamma is in most cases changed into a *w*.

The procedure is the following:

-ʾuʾ ➠ -ʾ(u)w

An example in which such a combination is carried out at the initial of the word is the passive voice of Form IV of *ʾaṯara* "to report" in the 3rd person of the masc. sing. formed according to *f(u)ūʿila,* namely *ʾuʾṯira* "it was reported" with the 2nd vowelless hamza preceded by a ḍamma. It becomes *ʾ(u)wṯira* with the hamza changed into a *w,* then as the vowelless *w* in it is preceded by a ḍamma, it becomes *ʾ(u)ūṯira* "he, or it was preferred /(passive)" with the *w* assimilated to the ḍamma resulting in the lengthened *ū.*

However it can be observed that in some cases of 1st radical hamzated verbs of the conjugation *faʿala yafʿulu* occurring in the imperative according to *ʾufʿul,* e.g. *ʾuʾḫuḏ* "take!" and *ʾuʾkul* "eat!" with the 2nd vowelless hamza preceded by the hamza of the imperative vowelled by a ḍamma, both hamzas are elided resulting respectively in *ḫuḏ* and *kul* (cf. Ibn Ǧinnī, *de Flexione* 33, Åkesson, *Ibn Masʿūd* 242: fol. 23a, Howell, II-III, 89-90, IV, fasc. I, 957-958, Wright, II, 76, Vernier, I, 103).

The elision of the hamza is obligatory in *ḫuḏ* which is not to be said *ʾuʾḫuḏ* with the combination of both hamzas, or *ʾuwḫuḏ* with the change of the 2nd hamza into a *w* resulting in *ʾu(ū)ḫuḏ,* and in *ku*l which is not to be said *ʾuʾkul, ʾuwkul* or *ʾ(u)ūkul.*

The procedure is then the following:

-ʾuʾ ➠ -

The elision however is not necessary in *mur* "order!" which is allowed, as well as in *ʾuwmur* in which the 1st hamza is maintained and the 1st radical hamza is changed into a *w* resulting in *ʾ(u)ūmur.*

Also *ʾamur* with the vowelling of the hamza with a fatḥa occurs as in the sur. 20: 132 *(wa-ʾamur ʾahlaka bi-l-ṣalwati)* "Enjoin prayer on thy people" and in the sur. 7: 199 *(wa-ʾamur bi-l-ᶜurfi ḫuḏi l-ᶜafwa)* "Hold to forgiveness; Command what is right".

1.1.2.7. The hamza and the hamza preceding it are vowelled by a fatḥa:

Two hamzas vowelled by a fatḥa combined together can occur in one word or in two words following each other.

The sequences that can be taken up are the following:

1.1.2.7.1. The hamza and the hamza preceding it are vowelled by a fatḥa in one word: their assimilation into a madda and the anomalous insertion of an *ā* in some cases.

1.1.2.7.2. The hamza is vowelled by a fatḥa in one word and follows a hamza vowelled by a fatḥa in the word preceding it: the elision of one hamza or of both.

1.1.2.7.1. The hamza and the hamza preceding it are vowelled by a fatha in one word: their assimilation into a madda and the anomalous insertion of an ā in some cases:

The possible assimilation of two hamzas vowelled by a fatḥa following each other at the beginning of the word concerns some examples in which the interrogative particle, *ʾa,* is prefixed in a word which has the conjunctive hamza vowelled by fatḥa of the definite *ʾal-* attached to it, e.g. *ʾa-ʾal-Ḥasanu ʿindaka* "Is al-Ḥasan by you?" which becomes *ʾ(a)āl-Ḥasanu ʿindaka* (cf. Howell, IV, fasc. I, 1003).

Hence the procedure is the following:

-ʾa-ʾa ➠ *-ʾ(a)ā*

The anomalous insertion of the *ā* in words in which the initial segment is the conjunctive hamza *ʾa,* to which the interrogative particle, *ʾa,* is prefixed to, can be remarked, e.g. *ʾa-ʾanti* "Are you /fem. sing.?" which becomes *ʾ(a)ā-ʾanti* (cf. Sībawaihi, II, 173, Åkesson, *Ibn Masʿūd* 242: fol. 23a).

Hence the procedure is the following:

-ʾa-ʾa ➠ *-ʾ(a)ā-ʾa*

As an example, the anomalous *ʾ(a)ā-ʾanti* that occurs in this part of a verse said by Ḏū l-Rumma, cited by Sībawaihi, II, 173, Ibn Ǧinnī, *Sirr II,* 723, Muʾaddib, *Taṣrīf* 32, Zamaḫšarī, 14, 167, Ibn Yaᶜīš, IX, 118-120, Howell, I, fasc. I, 119, IV, fasc. I, 982, Åkesson, *Ibn Masᶜūd* 262: (233) can be mentioned:

> *"Fa-yā ẓabyata l-waᶜsāʾi bayna ğulāğilin*
> *wa-bayna l-naqā ʾāʾanti ʾam ʾummu Sālimin"*
> "Then, O gazelle of the soft sandy ground
> between Ǧulāğil
> and the sand-hill, is this really you or Umm
> Sālim?".

1.1.2.7.2. The hamza is vowelled by a fatḥa in one word and follows a hamza vowelled by a fatḥa in the word preceding it: the elision of one hamza or of both:

Such a sequence occurs when the hamza vowelled by a fatḥa is the initial segment of a word and is preceded by a hamza vowelled by a fatḥa in the word preceding it (cf. Sībawaihi, II,

172, Zamaḫšarī, 167, Åkesson, *Ibn Masᶜūd* 242: fol. 23a, Howell, IV, fasc. I, 983-986).

An example is the sur. 47: 18 *(fa-qad ǧāʾa ʾašrāṭuhā)* "But already Have come some tokens", in which *ǧāʾa ʾašrāṭuhā* presents a combination of two hamzas vowelled by a fatḥa. Al-Ḫalīl and some other Arabs alleviate the 2nd hamza and not the1st one, and recite it as *fa-qad ǧāʾa šrāṭuhā* فَقَدْ جاءَ ٱشراطُها whereas the Ḥiǧāzīs alleviate both the hamzas by eliding the 1st one and changing the 2nd one into a *waṣla,* namely *fa-qad ǧā šrāṭuhā* فَقَدْ جا ٱشراطُها (cf. Åkesson, *Ibn Masᶜūd* 242: fol. 23a).

1.1.3. The hamza as the final segment of a word

The hamza as the final segment of a word can either be vowelled and preceded by a vowel (cf. 1.1.3.1.) or vowelled and preceded by a sukūn (cf. 1.1.3.2.). In the first case, the vowel preceding it determines which is the glide that supports it, and in the 2nd case the hamza is written on the line unsupported, unless if it concerns some anomalous cases found in some dialectal variants.

1.1.3.1. The vowelled hamza is preceded by a vowel:

It is not the hamza's own vowel that is the factor determining whether it is supported by a glide, - namely if it is written over or under the alif or over the *ʾu,* - because its vowel marks the inflection and varies according to the word's position in the sentence.

However it can be observed that it is the vowel preceding it that is the factor determining which is the glide that supports it (cf. Åkesson, *Ibn Masʿūd* 248: fol. 25a).

Examples are *qaraʾa* "to read" with the hamza written over the alif (قَرَأَ) on account of the fatḥa of the *r* preceding it, *ṭaruʾa* "to descend, to break in" with the hamza written over the *w* (طَرُؤَ) on account of the ḍamma of the *r* preceding it, and *fatiʾa* "not to cease to be, to refrain" with the hamza written over the *kursī l-yāʾ* (فَتِئَ) on account of the kasra of the *t* preceding it.

1.1.3.2. The vowelled hamza is preceded by a sukūn:

The vowelled segment that is preceded by a sukūn is written as a pure hamza on the line without being supported by any glide (cf. Åkesson, *Ibn Masʿūd* 248: fol. 25a-25b).

Some examples are *ḫab'un* "a hidden thing" (خَبْء) with the 1st radical given a fatḥa, *rid'un* "a buttress" (رِدْء) with the 1st radical given a kasra and *buṭ'un* "slowness" (بُطْء) with the 1st radical given a *ḍamma* (cf. Howell, IV, fasc. I, 807-812).

1.1.3.2.1. Some anomalous cases that concern the alleviation of the hamza:

The hamza in the examples *ḫab'un, rid'un* and *buṭ'un* is treated differently in the dialectal variants (for them see Howell, IV, fasc. I, 807-812).

The Ḥiǧāzīs elide it on account of the pause, and say in the definite form *al-ḫab, al-rid* and *al-buṭ.*

The Banū Tamīm give the 2nd radical a vowel that is similar to the vowel of the 1st radical and then change the hamza into a segment of the nature of the vowel preceding it by placing it over the glide, namely *al-ridi'* (الرِّدِئْ) and *al-buṭu'* (البُطُؤْ) in all the three cases of the nominative, accusative or genetive.

Some Arabs elide and do not shift the vowel of the hamza, and then change the hamza into an unsound segment homogeneous with its vowel, i.e. *al-ridw* (الرِّدْوْ) and *al-buṭw* (البُطْوْ).

Others shift the vowel of the hamza and change the 3rd radical into a glide, namely *al-ridiy* (الرِّدِي) and *al-buṭuw* (البُطُو).

2. THE CHANGES DUE TO THE WEAK CONSONANT

2.1. The soundness or the unsoundness of the weak consonant or glide

In the weak verbs and their forms, the weak consonant or glide can be sound or unsound. The sound glide is the one that is not subjected to any phonological change, e.g. *wa*^{c}*ada* "to promise", in which the *w* remains sound on the basis that it is not preceded by any other segment.

By contrast to the sound glide, the unsound one implies a change in the word structure, e.g. the imperfect *ya*^{c}*idu* underlyingly *yaw*^{c}*idu* in which the 1st radical *w* is elided.

The changes due to the unsoundness of the glide are termed as *ᵓiᶜlāl,* and the most common ones are: 1) that the unsound glide is made vowelless, 2) that it is changed into another glide, 3) that it is elided, 4) that its vowel is shifted, 5) or that it itself is shifted to the position of another segment (cf. Åkesson, *Ibn Masᶜūd* 270: fol. 25b-26a, Rāğiḥī, *Basīṭ* 159).

The weak verbs and their derivatives and the different sequences determing the soundness or unsoundness of the glide are taken up in this study.

A- The weak verbs

The glide is mostly found in the weak verbs and their derivatives. The unsoundness or *iᶜlāl* usually affects their structures. This is why the weak verb is designated as *muᶜtall* in Arabic, which means affected by an *iᶜlāl* or unsoundness.

The weak verbs fall into four categories, which refer to the position of the glide or glides in their structures. These are:

1- The verb with 1st *w* or y radical. It is generally termed as *muᶜtal al-fāᵓ* and also *al-miṯāl* "the assimilated verb".

2- The verb with 2nd radical *w* or *y* radical. It is generally termed as *muᶜtall al-ᶜayn* and also *al-ᵓağwaf* "the hollow verb".

3- The verb with 3rd radical *w* or *y* radical. It is generally termed as *mu*^{c}*tal al-lām* or the defective verb *al-nāqiṣ*.

4- The verb that is doubly weak. It is generally termed as *al-lafīf* "complicated, tangled".

Each of these categories have their specific classes and conjugations.

1- The conjugations of the verb with 1st radical w or *y:*

The verb with 1st *w* or y radical falls into two classes: verbs with 1st radical *w* and verbs with 1st radical *y*.

a- The conjugation of the verb with 1st radical w:

1- *fa*^{c}*ala yaf*^{c}*ilu,* e.g. *wa*^{c}*ada yaw*^{c}*idu* "to promise", of which the imperfect *yaw*^{c}*idu* becomes after the phonological change *ya*^{c}*idu* with the 1st radical *w* elided.

2- *fa*^{c}*ala yaf*^{c}*alu,* e.g. *wahaba yawhabu* "to give", of which the imperfect *yawhabu* becomes after the phonological change *yahabu* with the 1st radical *w* elided.

3- *fa^{c}ila yaf^{c}alu,* e.g. *wağila yawğalu* "to be afraid", of which the 1st radical *w* is maintained in the imperfect *yawğalu.*

4- *fa^{c}ila yaf^{c}ilu,* e.g. *wamiqa yawmiqu* "to love", of which the imperfect *yawmiqu* becomes after the phonological change *yamiqu* with the 1st radical *w* elided.

5- *fa^{c}ula yaf^{c}ulu,* e.g. *wabula yawbulu* "to be unwholesome", of which the 1st radical *w* is maintained in the imperfect *yawbulu.*

The example *wa^{c}ada* "to promise" becomes *ya^{c}idu* in the imperfect of the indicative active. Its imperative is *^{c}id,* its active participle is *wā^{c}idun,* its *maṣdar* is *wa^{c}dun* or *^{c}idatun,* its perfect passive is *wu^{c}ida,* its imperfect is *yū^{c}adu* and its passive participle is *maw^{c}ūdun.*

b- The conjugation of the verb with 1st radical y:

The conjugations of the verb with 1st radical *y* can conveniently be grouped into the following ones:

1- *fa^{c}ala yaf^{c}ilu,* e.g. *yana^{c}a yayni^{c}u* "to become ripe", of which the imperfect is inflected as the strong verb, namely *yayni^{c}u* or *yayna^{c}u.*

2- *faᶜala yafᶜalu,* e.g. *yafaᶜa yayfaᶜu* "to be grown up", of which the imperfect is inflected as the strong verb, namely *yayfaᶜu.*

3- *faᶜila yafᶜalu,* e.g. *yaqiẓa yayqaẓu* "to be awake", of which the imperfect is inflected as the strong verb, namely *yayqaẓu.*

4- *faᶜula yafᶜulu,* e.g. *yaquẓa yayquẓu* "to be awake", of which the imperfect is inflected as the strong verb, namely *yayquẓu.*

The example *yasara* "to be easy" becomes *yaysiru* in the imperfect of the indicative active. Its imperative is *ᵓiysir* > *ᵓīsir,* its active participle is *yāsirun,* its *maṣdar* is *yasrun,* its passive is *yusira,* its imperfect is *yūsaru* and its passive participle is *maysūrun.*

<u>*2- The conjugations of the verb with 2nd radical w* or *y:*</u>

The verb with 2nd *w* or y radical falls into two classes: verbs with 2nd radical *w* and verbs with 2nd radical *y.*

<u>*a- The conjugations of the verb with 2nd radical w:*</u>

The conjugations of the verb with 2nd radical *w* can be grouped into the following:

1- *faᶜala yafᶜulu,* e.g. *qawala yaqwulu* that becomes after the phonological change *qāla yaqūlu* "to say".

2- *faᶜila yafᶜalu,* e.g. *ḫawifa yaḫwafu* that becomes after the phonological change *ḫāfa yaḫāfu* "to fear".

3- *faᶜula yafᶜulu,* e.g. *ṭawula yaṭwulu* that becomes after the phonological change *ṭāla yaṭūlu* "to become long".

The example of *qāla* "to ask" becomes *yaqūlu* in the imperfect of the indicative active. Its imperative is *qul,* its active participle is *qāʾilun,* its *maṣdar* is *qawlun,* its perfect passive is *qīla,* its imperfect is *yuqālu* and its passive participle is *maqūlun.*

b- The conjugations of the verb with 2nd radical y:

The conjugations of the verb with 2nd radical *y* can be grouped into the following:

1- *faᶜala yafᶜilu,* e.g. *bayaᶜa yabyiᶜu* that becomes after the phonological change *bāᶜa yabīᶜu* "to sell".

2- *faᶜila yafᶜalu,* e.g. *hayiba yahyabu* that becomes after the phonological change *hāba yahābu* "to fear".

The example *bāᶜa* "to buy" becomes *yabīᶜu* in the imperfect of the indicative active. Its imperative is *biᶜ,* its active participle is *bāʾiᶜun,* its *maṣdar* is *bayᶜun,* its perfect passive is *bīᶜa,* its imperfect is *yubāᶜu* and its passive participle is *mabīᶜun.*

3- The conjugations of the verb with 3rd radical w or *y:*

The verb with 3rd *w* or y radical falls into two classes: verbs with 3rd radical *w* and verbs with 3rd radical *y.*

a- The conjugations of the verb with 3rd radical w:

The verb with 3rd radical *w* falls into the following conjugation:

1- *faᶜala yafᶜulu,* e.g. *ġazawa yaġzuwu* "to attack" that becomes after the phonological change *ġazā yaġzū.*

The example of a verb with 3rd radical *w* in the perfect is *ġazā* "to attack" (with final *alif mamdūda).* It becomes *yaġzū* in the imperfect of the indicative active. Its imperative is *ʾuġzu,* its active participle is *ġāzin,* its *maṣdar* is *ġazwun,* its perfect passive is *ġuziya,* its imperfect is *yuġzā* and its passive participle is *maġzīyun.*

b- The conjugations of the verb with 3rd radical b:

The verb with 3rd radical *y* falls into the following conjugations:

1- *fa^{c}ala yaf^{c}ilu,* e.g. *ramaya yarmiyu* "to throw" that becomes after the phonological change *ramā yarmī.*

2- *fa^{c}ala yaf^{c}alu,* e.g. *nahaya yanhayu* "to forbid" that becomes after the phonological change *nahā yanhā.*

3- *fa^{c}ila yaf^{c}alu,* e.g. *raḍiya yarḍayu* "to consent" that becomes after the phonological change *raḍā yarḍā.*

The example *ramaya* "to throw" becomes *yarmī* in the imperfect of the indicative active. Its imperative is *ʾirmi,* its active participle is *rāmin,* its *maṣdar* is *ramyun,* its perfect passive is *rumiya,* its imperfect is *yurmā,* its passive participle is *marmīyun* and the nouns of time and place are *marman.*

4- The conjugations of the doubly weak verbs:

The doubly weak verb is divid is divided into two classes:

1- *mafrūq:* having a 1st and 3rd weak radical, e.g. *waq(a)ā yaq(i)y* "to guard, preserve".

2- *maqrūn:* having a 2nd and 3rd weak radical, e.g. *ṭaw(a)ā yaṭw(i)y* "to fold".

a- The conjugations of the mafrūq or verb with 1st and 3rd weak radical:

1- *fa^{c}ala yaf^{c}ilu,* e.g. *waqaya yaqiyu* that becomes after the phonological change *waq(a)ā* [with final *alif maqṣūra] yaq(i)ī* "to guard, preserve".

2- *fa^{c}ila yaf^{c}ilu,* e.g. *waliya yaliyu* "to be near" of which only the imperfect becomes after the phonological change *yal(i)ī.*

3- *fa^{c}ila yaf^{c}alu,* e.g. *wağiya yawğayu* of which only the imperfect becomes after the phonological change *yawğ(a)ā* [with final *alif maqṣūra].*

The example *waq(a)ā* "he guarded" becomes *yaqī* in the imperfect of the indicative active. Its imperative is *qi* or *qih,* its active participle is *wāqin,* its *maṣdar* is *waqyun,* its perfect passive is *wuqiya,* its imperfect is *yūqā,* its passive participle is *mawqīyun,* its noun of place is *mawqan* and its noun of instrument is *mīqan.*

b- The conjugations of the maqrūn or verb with 2nd and 3rd weak radicals:

1- *fa^{c}ala yaf^{c}ilu,* e.g. *ṭawaya yaṭwiyu* that becomes after the phonological change ṭawā [with final *alif maqṣūra] yaṭwī* "to fold".

2- *fa^{c}ila yaf^{c}alu,* e.g. *qawiya yaqwayu* "to be strong" of which only the imperfect becomes after the phonological change *yaqwā* [with final *alif maqṣūra].*

3- *fa^{c}ila yaf^{c}alu,* e.g. *ḥayiya yaḥyayu* of which only the imperfect becomes after the phonological change *yaḥyā* [with final *alif mamdūda].*

The example *ṭawā* [with final *alif maqṣūra]* "he folded" becomes *yaṭwī* in the imperfect of the indicative active. Its imperative is *ʾiṭwi,* its active participle is *ṭāwin,* its *maṣdar* is *ṭayyun,* its perfect passive is *ṭuwiya,* its imperfect is *yuṭwā,* its passive participle is *maṭwīyun,* its noun of place is *maṭwan* and its noun of instrument is *miṭwan.*

C- The sequences involved for the soundness or unsoundness of the glide:

In words beginning with a weak consonant, the weak consonant remains usually sound in them. An example is *wa^{c}ada* "to promise", in which the *w* remains sound on the basis that it is not preceded by any other segment. This rule implies that no phonological change can affect the initial segment. Hence, this means that the *w* in *wa^{c}ada* cannot be made vowelless resulting in *w^{c}ada,* because of the impossibility of beginning the word with a vowelless segment. It could not either be changed into *ā* resulting in *ā*^{c}*ada* as this would imply beginning the word with a vowelless segment which is forbidden, and it could not either be elided as the root would seem to be formed of two radicals, i.e. ^{c}*ada,* which is not allowed (cf. Åkesson, *Ibn Mas*^{c}*ūd* 270: fol. 25b-26a).

Other examples of verbs with the weak 1st radical retained in the perfect, are: *wahaba* "he gave", *wağila* "he was afraid", *wamiqa* "he loved", *wabula* "he was unwholesome".

It can be stated however, that the 1st weak radical can be elided in some cases of verbal nouns, e.g. ^{c}*idatun* underlyingly *wi*^{c}*dun* "a promise" (for some examples see Suyūṭī, *Muzhir II,* 158-159), in spite of the fact that it is the initial segment of the word. This opposes the rule that the glide should be preceded by another segment if a phonological change is to be carried out. The breaking of this rule requests however that the *tā*^{ɔ} *marbūṭa* is suffixed to the word as a compensation for the elision of this initial glide (cf. Sībawaihi, II, 81, Wright, II, 118, Lane, II, 2952).

Not only the *tā*^{ɔ} *marbūṭa* can occur as a compensation of a glide in the same word, but also another word, occurring as the 2nd element of an ^{ɔ}*iḍāfa* construction, can occur as a compensation for the elision of a *tā*^{ɔ} *marbūṭa.* As an example to be mentioned, the *tā*^{ɔ} *marbūṭa* is anomalously elided from the accusative *ᶜidata* which is said *ᶜida,* when it occurs as the first element of a construct state in this verse said by Abū Umayya al-Faḍl b. al-ᶜAbbās b. ᶜUtba b. Abī Lahab, that is cited by Ibn Ǧinnī, *Ḫaṣāʾiṣ III,* 171, Muʾaddib, *Taṣrīf* 285, Suyūṭī, *Ašbāh III,* 248, Ibn Manẓūr, VI, 4871, Howell, I, fasc. IV, 1527-1528, IV, fasc. I, 1423-1424, Åkesson, *Ibn Masᶜūd* 277: (248):

> *"ʾInna l-ḫalīṭa ʾaǧaddū l-bayna fa-nǧara*
> *wa-ʾaḫlafūka ᶜida l-ʾamri l-laḏī waᶜadū".*
> "Verily the familiar friends have renewed the
> separation, and made off,
> and have broken to you the promise of the
> matter which they promised".

There exist two different theories concerning the elision of the *tāʾ marbūṭa* from *ᶜidatun* and its likes. One of them is Sībawaihi's theory (cf. Sībawaihi, II, 260-261) who accepts the elision of the *tāʾ marbūṭa* even when the word to which it is suffixed is not the first element of a construct state, and the other one is al-Farrāʾs, who can only accept this elision when the word is the first element of the construct state, as in the case of *ᶜida l-ʾamri* of this verse, as he considers the second element of the construct, namely *l-ʾamri,* as a compensation for the elided *tāʾ marbūṭa* (cf. Muʾaddib, *Taṣrīf* 285, Åkesson, *Ibn Masᶜūd* 270-272: fol. 26a).

The soundness of the glide or the phonological change(s) due to its unsoundness involves a sequence of two segments in which the unsound glide is the second segment and is preceded by a vowelless or a vowelled sound segment. It goes without saying that the sequence of two vowelless segments is excluded, as it is impossible to combine two vowelless segments together.

In order to have a system of analysis that makes it possible to explore the phonological changes, the following sequences comprising a glide preceded by a sound segment, whether strong or weak, are presented and analyzed:

2.1.1. The glide is vowelless and preceded by a fatḥa: its soundness or its change into an *ā*.

2.1.2. The glide is vowelled by a fatḥa and preceded by a fatḥa: its change into an *ā*.

2.1.3. The glide is vowelled by a kasra and preceded by a fatḥa: its change into an *ā*.

2.1.4. The glide is vowelled by a ḍamma and preceded by a fatḥa: the change of the *wu* or *yu* into an *ā*.

2.1.5. The glide, the *y*, is vowelless and preceded by a ḍamma: its change into a *w*.

2.1.6. The glide is vowelled by a kasra and preceded by a ḍamma: the transfer of the kasra to the preceding segment and hence the change of the preceding segment's ḍamma into a kasra, the change of the *w* into a *y* or the *y* into an *ī* respectively, or the elision of the glide's kasra and the lengthening of the ḍamma preceding it into an *ū*.

2.1.7. The glide is vowelled by a ḍamma and preceded by a vowel: the glide's ḍamma is elided.

2.1.8. The glide is vowelled by a fatḥa and preceded by a ḍamma: its soundness.

2.1.9. The glide, the *w,* is vowelled by a fatḥa and preceded by a kasra: its change into a *y.*

2.1.10. The glide, the *y,* is vowelled by a ḍamma and preceded by a kasra: the transfer of the ḍamma before the *y* and hence the change of the preceding segment's kasra into a ḍamma, the elision of the *y* and the lengthening of the ḍamma into an *ū* according to a theory, or the elision of the *y's* ḍamma together with the elision of the *y* and the change of the preceding segment's kasra into a ḍamma according to another theory.

2.1.11. The glide, the *y,* is vowelled by a kasra and preceded by a kasra: the elision of the vowel of the *y* together with the *y.*

2.1.12. The glide is vowelled by a fatḥa and preceded by a sukūn: the transfer of the fatḥa to the segment preceding it and the change of the *w* into an *ā*.

2.1.13. The glide, the *y*, is vowelled by a kasra and preceded by a sukūn: the transfer of the kasra to the segment preceding it and the change of the *y* into an *ī*.

2.1.14. The glide is vowelled by a kasra and preceded by a vowelless *ā:* the change of the *wi* or *yi* into *ʾi*.

2.1.15. The glide, the *w*, is vowelled by a ḍamma and preceded by a sukūn: the transfer of the ḍamma to the segment preceding it and the change of the *w* into *ū*.

2.1.16. The glide, the *y*, is vowelled by a ḍamma and preceded by a sukūn: the transfer of the ḍamma to the vowelless segment preceding it, the change of the ḍamma into a kasra and the change of the *y* into *ī*.

2.1.17. The glide, the *w* or *y*, is vowelless and preceded by a kasra: its change into a *y* or *ī* respectively.

2.1.18. The transposition of segments in some nouns.

It shall be remarked concerning these sequences that some of them are affected by a change or a series of changes due to the unsoundness of the glides in them whereas others are not.

D- Conditions for the phonological change due to the unsoundness of the glide:

There exist as well some conditions (cf. Howell, IV, fasc. I, 1237 sqq. who discusses eleven conditions, Bohas/Kouloughli, *Linguistic* 85-86 who discuss three) that are to be followed if a phonological change is carried out due to the unsoundness of the glide. I can mention seven common ones here:

1 - the glide should be in a verb or in a noun of the verbal form of the measure *faᶜal*. This is why the phonological change is not carried out if the pattern has the *tāᵓ marbūṭa* or the *alif maqṣūra* suffixed to it. Some examples are *ḥawakatun* "weavers" that did not become *ḥ(a)ākatun* and *Ṣawar(a)ā* "*Ṣawar(a)ā,* name of a water" that did not become *Ṣ(a)ār(a)ā* (for discussions see 2.1.2.2.1.: 1).

The phonological change is not either carried out if the word is formed according to a certain form, and hence is not formed according to *faᶜal.* Some examples are *ǧadwalun* "a rivulet" that is formed according to *faᶜwalun* and *miqwalun* "loquacious, eloquent" and *miḫyaṭun* "a needle" that are formed according to the contracted form *mifᶜalun* of *mifᶜ(a)ālun* (for discussions see 2.1.12.1.: 1).

2 - The glide should not be vowelled by a vowel that is not supplied by the basic form. An example is *daᶜaw(u) l-qawma*

(دَعَوُا ٱلْقَوْمَ) "they called for the people" in which the sequence *w(u)* is retained because the *u* is a vowel of juncture given to the *w* to avoid the cluster of the underlying vowelless *w* of *da*ᶜ*aw* (دَعَوْا) with the vowelless *l*- following the *waṣla* in the definite article prefixed to the second word *l-qawma* (for discussions see 2.1.4.1.: 1).

Another example is *al-dalwu* "the bucket" in which the *w* remains sound as its vowel marks the declension in a certain sentence (cf. 2.1.15.1. :1) and *al-ramyu* "the throwing" in which the *y* remains sound for the same reason (for discussions see par. 2.1.16.1.: 1).

3 - The fatḥa or the kasra preceding the glide is ruled by the sukūn of another form. An example with the fatḥa vowelling the *w* is Form VIII *ᵓiǧtawar(u)ū* "they became mutual neighbours" that did not become *ᵓiǧt(a)ār(u)ū* because it has the meaning of Form VI *taǧ(a)āwar(u)ū* (for discussions see 2.1.2.1.1.: 2.) in which the sukūn of the *ā* prevented the sequence *wa* after it to be changed into an *ā*. Hence it is as if this *ā* rules as well the sequence *wa* in *ᵓiǧtawar(u)ū.* An example with the kasra vowelling the *w* is Form I *ᶜawira* "to be blind of one eye" that did not become *ᶜ(a)āra,* because it is associated to Form IX *ᵓiᶜwarra,* in which the sukūn of the consonant ᶜ hindered any change to affect the sequence *wa* (for discussions see 2.1.3.1.:

1.). Hence it is as if this vowelless ^{c} rules as well the sequence *wi* in ^{c}*awira,* and hence hinders any change to affect it.

4 - The word refers in its meaning to intensive mobility. An example is *ḥayaw(a)ānun* "animal, much life" that did not become *ḥ(a)āw(a)ānun* (for discussions see 2.1.2.2.1.: 3.).

5- The combination of two phonological changes due to the unsound glides should be avoided. An example is *ṭawaya* that becomes *ṭaw(a)ā* [with final *alif maqṣūra]* "to fold" with one phonological change, and should not result in *ṭ(a]ā(a)ā* with a second phonological change carried out in it (for discussions see 2.1.2.1.1.: 1.).

6- The form should remain unchanged to prevent that the last glide becomes vowelled by a ḍamma in the imperfect. An example is *ḥayiya* "to live" that did not become *ḥ(a)āya,* to avoid that its imperfect becomes *yaḥ(a)āyu* (for discussions see 2.1.3.1. 2).

7- The glide is meant to give clues to the base form. Some examples are *qawadun* "retaliation" with the *wa* retained that refers to the root *q w d* and *ṣayadun* "a disease in a camel's head" with the *ya* retained that refers to the root *s y d* (for discussions see 2.1.2.2.1.: 2).

2.1.1. The glide is vowelless and preceded by a fatḥa: its soundness or its change into an ā:

The glide, the *w* or the *y,* which is vowelless and preceded by a fatḥa is mostly sound, and is therefore not changed into an *ā* unless in some anomalous cases. Hence the rule is the following:

-aw → *-aw*

-ay → *-ay*

Some examples are the verbal nouns of verbs with 2nd weak radical formed according to *fa*^{c}*lun,* e.g. *qawlun* "a saying" with the 2nd radical *w* retained and *bay*^{c}*un* "a selling" with the 2nd radical *y* retained. Some prefer however to consider the *w* in *qawlun* as unsound and change it anomalously into an *ā,* i.e. *q(a)ālun* (cf. Ibn Manẓūr, V, 3779, Åkesson, *Ibn Mas*^{c}*ūd* 282: fol. 27a), but the variant pertains to the anomalies.

The reason of the soundness of the glide is that the fatḥa preceding it, which is followed by the sukūn, is not considered as a strong vowel capable of forcing a change upon it (cf. Åkesson, *Ibn Mas*^{c}*ūd* 282: fol. 27a).

Another case in which the weak radical is retained is the verb with 3rd radical *w* or *y* in the perfect, in which the 3rd weak radical is vowelless and precedes the vowelled agent pronoun suffix, e.g. *da*^{c}*aw-tu* "I called", and hence *da*^{c}*aw-ta* "you called /masc. sing.", *da*^{c}*aw-ti* "you called /fem. sing." and *da*^{c}*aw-na* "they called /fem. pl.", and *ramay-tu* "I threw", - and hence *ramay-ta* "you threw /masc. sing.", *ramay-ti* "you threw /fem. sing." and *ramay-na* "they called /fem. pl.", respectively.

As what concerns the case in which the vowelless *w* or the *y* preceded by a fatḥa is changed into an *ā,* it can be remarked that it is carried out as the second step of a phonological change that implies at first the transfer of a vowel. This is the case of the imperfect of the verb with 2nd radical *w* vowelled by a fatḥa that occurs formed according to the conjugation *yaf*^{c}*alu,* e.g. *yaḫwafu* > *yaḫawfu* > *yaḫ(a)āfu* "he is afraid" and of the verb with 2nd radical *y,* e.g. *yahyabu* > *yahaybu* > *yah(a)ābu* "he is afraid".

2.1.1.1. Some anomalous cases:

In spite of the fact that the *w* is preceded by a fatḥa, it can be changed into a *y* anomalously in some cases:

-aw ➠ *-ay*

This occurs in the derived forms of perfects of some verbs with with 3rd radical *w,* e.g. Form II *ġazzawa* that becomes *ġazzaya* "to raid" and then *ġazz(a)ā* [with final *alif maqṣūra],*

Form IV *ʾaġzaw-tu* > *ʾaġzay-tu* "I raided" and Form X *ʾistarḍawa* > *ʾistarḍaya* > *ʾistarḍ(a)ā*.

The change of the *w* into a *y* in these forms is on the analogy of its change into a *y* in their imperfects: Form II *yuġazziwu* > *yuġazziyu* "he raids", Form IV *yuġziwu* > *yuġz(i)yu* > *yuġz(i)ī* "he raids" and Form X *yastarḍiwu* > *yastarḍiyu* > *yastarḍ(i)ī* (cf. Wright, II, 91).

2.1.2. The glide is vowelled by a fatḥa and preceded by a fatḥa: its change into an ā:

This sequence occurs in verbs with 2nd or 3rd weak radical and in nouns and adjectives. As it is remarked below, the glide is changed into an *ā* in verbs with 2nd weak radical (cf. 2.1.2.1) and in nouns and adjectives (cf. 2.1.2.2.), and into an *alif mamdūda* in verbs with 3rd radical *w* or into an *alif maqṣūra* in verbs with 3rd radical *y* (cf. 2.1.2.1). The glide remains sound in some specific cases (cf. 2.1.2.1.1.).

2.1.2.1. The phonological change that is carried out in verbs:

The cases that can be mentioned are the perfects of verbs with 2nd or 3rd weak radical in the 3rd person of the masc. sing.

In the cases of verbs with 2nd weak radical, the glide, the *w* or the *y*, is vowelled by a fatḥa and is preceded by one, which results in its change into an *ā*.

-awa ➠ *- (a)ā*

-aya ➠ *- (a)ā*

An example of a verb with weak 2nd radical *w* is *qawala* > *q(a)āla* "to say".

An example of a verb with weak 2nd radical *y* is *baya^{c}a* > *b(a)ā^{c}a* "to sell".

In the cases of verbs with 3rd weak radical, the glide, the *w* or the *y*, is vowelled by a fatḥa and preceded by one, which results in its change into an *alif mamdūda* if the glide is a *w*, e.g. *ġazawa* > *ġaz(a)ā* "to raid" [with final *alif mamdūda]* or into an *alif maqṣūra* if the glide is a *y*, e.g. *ramaya* > *ram(a)ā* "to throw".

2.1.2.1.1. The soundness of the glide:

The glide remains sound in these cases that are discussed below, just to mention a few:

1- The combination of two phonological changes due to the unsound glides should be avoided.

2- The fatḥa preceding the glide is ruled by the sukūn of another form.

1- The combination of two phonological changes due to the unsound glides should be avoided:

An example that can introduce two phonological changes, which is forbidden, is *ṭawaya* in which the sequence *ya* preceded by a fatḥa is changed into an *(a)ā,* namely *ṭaw(a)ā* [with final *alif maqṣūra]* "to fold" (cf. Åkesson, *Ibn Mas*^{c}*ūd* 284: fol. 28a). It is not allowed after this change to change the sequence *wa* of *ṭaw(a)ā* preceded by a fatḥa into *(a)ā* that would result in *ṭ(a)āā* as this would necessarily imply a cluster of two vowelless glides, the alifs: the *alif mamdūda* and the *alif maqṣūra.*

It can be remarked that the phonological change is not carried out as well in the dual of the masc. *ṭaway(a)ā* "/dual" in spite of the fact that the final radical *y* is vowelled, and thus there is no risk in combining two vowelless segments, by analogy with *ṭaw(a)ā* (cf. ibid, 284: fol. 28a). In other words *ṭaway(a)ā* could have become *ṭ(a)āy(a)ā,* but did not do so by analogy with *ṭaw(a)ā* that did not either become *ṭ(a)āā.*

2- The fatḥa preceding the glide is ruled by the sukūn of another form:

A factor that can hinder the change of the glide vowelled by a fatḥa and preceded by one into an *ā,* is that the fatḥa of the segment preceding the glide in a specific form can be influenced theoretically by the sukūn of another form which it resembles in meaning, and thus this fatḥa is counted as ruled by a sukūn (cf. ibid, 284: fol. 27b-28a).

This is the case of some verbs of Form VIII *ʾiftaᶜala* with 2nd radical *w,* that have the meaning of Form VI *taf(a)āᶜala* denoting the reciprocity, in which the *w* is counted as sound in them (cf. Sībawaihi, II, 399-401, Zamaḫšarī, 180, Ibn Yaᶜīš, X, 74-75, Howell, II-III, 275, IV, fasc. I, 1242-1243), and thus the sequence *awa* in them is not changed into *(a)ā.* Some examples are Form VIII *ʾiǧtawar(u)ū* "they became mutual neighbours" that did not become *ʾiǧt(a)ār(u)ū* because it has the meaning of Form VI *taǧ(a)āwar(u)ū,* and Form VIII *ʾizdawaǧ(u)ū* "they intermarried" that did not become *ʾizd(a)āǧ(u)ū* because it has the meaning of Form VI *taz(a)āwaǧ(u)ū.* The change of the sequence awa into *(a)ā* is necessary otherwise, e.g. *ʾiḫtawana* that has the meaning of Form I *ḫ(a)āna,* which becomes *ʾiḫt(a)āna* "was unfaithful".

To be more explicit, in for instance the case of Form VIII *ʾiǧtawara,* the fatḥa preceding the *w* is counted as being ruled by the sukūn of the vowelless *ā* preceding the *w* in Form VI *taǧ(a)āwara* (cf. Åkesson, *Ibn Mas^cūd* 284: fol. 28a), which is the reason why the *wa* is retained and the form did not become *ᵓiǧt(a)āra.* As a matter of fact, *ᵓiǧtawara* is associated to *taǧ(a)āwara* on account of its similarity of meaning to it, and in *taǧ(a)āwara,* the vowelless *ā* prevented the change of the sequence *wa* into *(a)ā.* It is then as if the vowelless *ā* of *taǧ(a)āwara* rules as well the *w* of *ᵓiǧtawara,* in which the fatḥa becomes counted as a sukūn, and thus hinders any change to be carried out.

2.1.2.2. The phonological change that is carried out in nouns and adjectives:

The phonological change is carried out in the noun or adjective on the condition that the noun is formed according to the verbal form *fa^cal.*

-awa ➠ *-(a)ā*

An example is *dawarun* with the 2nd radical *w* vowelled by a fatḥa and preceded by one that becomes *d(a)ārun* "house" after that the *wa* is changed into an *ā.*

The phonological change that is carried out in this noun is not only due to the fact that its glide is vowelled by a fatḥa and is preceded by one, but also because it answers the condition of resembling the verbal form *fa^{c}al* (for this condition see Åkesson, *Ibn Mas^{c}ūd* 284: fol. 27b, Bohas/Kouloughli, *Linguistic* 86). Thus no phonological change is carried out in nouns that lose their resemblance to a verbal form through the suffixation of a noun suffix (cf. 2.1.2.2.1.: 1).

2.1.2.2.1. The soundness of the glide:

The glide remains sound in the noun or in the adjective in the following cases that are discussed below, just to mention a few:

1- The noun or the adjective is not formed according to the verbal form *fa^{c}al* through the suffixation of the *tā^{ɔ} marbūṭa* or the *alif maqṣūra*.

2- The glide is meant to give clues to the base form.

3- The word refers in its meaning to intensive mobility.

1- The noun or the adjective is not formed according to the verbal form faᶜal through the sufixation of the tāᵓ marbūṭa or the alif maqṣūra:

Some examples are *ḥawakatun* "weavers", which is the pl. of *ḥ(a)āᵓikun* and *ḫawanatun* "traitors", which is the pl. of *ḫ(a)āᵓinun* (cf. Zamaḫšarī, 181, Åkesson, *Ibn Masᶜūd* 284: fol. 28a, Howell, IV, fasc. I, 1510). Both these triliterals differ from their verbs' measures *ḥawaka* "to weave" and *ḫawana* "to betray" through the *tāᵓ marbūṭa* of feminization. This is the reason why the sequence *wa* is not changed into *(a)ā* in them, and serves through its retaining to give indication of their base forms.

An example of a noun to which the *alif maqṣūra* is suffixed to is *Ṣawar(a)ā* "Ṣawar(a)ā, name of a water" (cf. Åkesson, *Ibn Masᶜūd* 284: fol. 28a), which is referred to as being the name of a water in Medīna (cf. Ibn Wallād, *Maqṣūr* 74). The sequence *wa* in it is retained and not changed into an *ā.*

An example of an adjective is *ḥayad(a)ā* "(a he-ass) shying at his own shadow because of his liveliness" (cf. Åkesson, *Ibn Masᶜūd* 284: fol. 28a, Howell, IV, fasc. I, 1251), that is formed according to the pattern *faᶜal(a)ā,* in which the *ya* is retained.

2- The glide is meant to give clues to the base form:

An example of a noun in which the *w* is intended to notify of the base form is *qawadun* "retaliation" that refers to the root *q w d*, and of a noun in which the *y* is intended to notify of the base form is *ṣayadun* "a disease in a camel's head" (cf. Zamaḫšarī, 173, Åkesson, *Ibn Mas*ᶜ*ūd* 284: fol. 28a, Howell, IV, fasc. I, 1251) that refers to *s y d*. The sequence *wa* in *qawadun* is not changed into *(a)ā*, i.e. *qa(ā)dun*, in spite of its being vowelled with a fatḥa and preceded by one, as this would cause a confusion on whether the form is from the root *qawada* "to lead" with the *w* as 2nd radical or the root *qayada* "to bind" with the *y* as 2nd radical.

The same goes for the *ya* in *ṣayadun* that is not changed into *(a)ā*, i.e. *ṣa(ā)dun*, as this would cause a confusion on whether the form is from the root *ṣawada* with the *w* as 2nd radical, that is the base form of *al-ṣ(a)ādu* "the [letter] ṣād" or the root *ṣayada* "to hunt" with the *y* as 2nd radical.

3- The word refers in its meaning to intensive mobility:

This is the case of the noun ḥ*ayaw(a)ānun* "animal, much life" (cf. Åkesson, *Ibn Mas*ᶜ*ūd* 284: fol. 28a, Howell, IV, fasc.

I, 1409) in which no phonological change is carried out so that the word corresponds in mobility to what it represents, which is a mobile animal. It occurs in the sur. 29: 64 *(la-hya l-ḥayawānu)* "that is Life indeed".

The variant *mawt(a)ānun* is its opposite in meaning, and on this account it is formed according to its pattern (cf. Ibn Manẓūr, VI, 4296, Åkesson, *Ibn Mas*^{c}*ūd* 284: fol. 28a, Lane, I, 679, 682, Howell, IV, fasc. I, 1244, 1409, 1465).

2.1.3. The glide is vowelled by a kasra and preceded by a fatḥa: its change into an ā:

The glide that is vowelled by a kasra and preceded by a fatḥa is changed into an *ā*.

-awi → *-(a)ā*

-ayi → *-(a)ā*

The cases that can be mentioned are the perfects of verbs with 2nd weak radical in the 3rd person of the masc. sing. of the conjugation *fa*^{c}*ila.*

An example of a verb with weak 2nd radical *w* vowelled by a kasra is *ḫawifa* > *ḫ(a)āfa* "to fear".

An example of a verb with 2nd radical *y* vowelled by a kasra is *hayiba* > *h(a)āba* "to be afraid".

2.1.3.1. The soundness of the glide:

The glide remains sound in these cases that are discussed below, just to mention a few:

1- The fatḥa preceding the glide is ruled by the sukūn of another form.

2- The form should remain unchanged to prevent that the last glide becomes vowelled by a ḍamma in the imperfect.

1- The fatha preceding the glide is ruled by the sukūn of another form:

The same procedure is applied as the one that concerns the verb with the 2nd radical vowelled by a fatḥa and preceded by one, e.g. Form VIII *ʾiğtawar(u)ū* "they became mutual neighbours" in which the *w* remains sound as the fatḥa preceding it is ruled by the sukūn of the *ā* of Form VI *tağ(a)āwar(u)ū* (cf. 2.1.2.1.1.: 2).

An example with the glide vowelled by a kasra and preceded by a fatḥa is Form I *ᶜawira* "to be blind of one eye". In this example the sequence *wi* did not become *a(ā)* as expected due to the influence of the fatḥa preceding it, which would result in *ᶜ(a)āra,* because the verb is associated to Form IX *ᵓiᶜwarra* with which it shares the same meaning. As the sukūn of the consonant *ᶜ* in *ᵓiᶜwarra* hinders any change to affect the sequence *wa,* it is as if this sukūn rules as well the *ᶜa* in Form I *ᶜawira,* and by doing so, hinders the change to be carried out in the sequence *wi* that could have resulted in *ᶜ(a)āra.*

Another example of a verb is *ḥawila* "squinted", which has the meaning of Form IX *ᵓiḥwalla,* and for the same reason as with *ᶜawira* has the sequence *wi* unchanged (cf. Sībawaihi, II, 399, Zamaḫšarī, 180, Howell, IV, fasc. I, 1241-1242). It can be noted that Wright, *Comparative Grammar* 243 was perplexed by the uncontraction in *ᶜawira* and *ḥawila,* as he writes:

> "I do not know why *ḫawifa* became *ḫāfa,* and *mawita, māta,* whilst *ḥawila* and *ᶜawira* remained uncontracted".

2- The form should remain unchanged to prevent that the last glide becomes vowelled by a ḍamma in the imperfect:

This is the case of *ḥayiya* "to live" (cf. Åkesson, *Ibn Masᶜūd* 284: fol. 28a) in which the sequence *yi* is not changed into *(a)ā* due to the influence of the fatḥa preceding it, namely *ḥ(a)āya,* to avoid that its imperfect becomes *yaḥ(a)āyu,* with the disliked combination of the ḍamma following the *y* that is deemed as heavy (cf. Åkesson, *Conversion* 28). Instead the imperfect is *yaḥy(a)ā* [with final *alif maqṣūra].*

It can be remarked that *yaḥy(a)ā* with the *alif mamdūda* substituted for the *alif maqṣūra* occurs instead of *yaḥy(a)ā* (with the *alif maqsūra),* in e.g. the sur. 8: 44 *(wa-yaḥyā man ḥayya ᶜan bayyinatin)* "And those who lived might live after a Clear Sign". As for the reason of this substitution it is to distinguish the imperfect from the proper name *Yaḥyā* (with *alif maqṣūra)* "John".

2.1.4. The glide is vowelled by a ḍamma and preceded by a fatḥa: the change of the wu or yu into an ā:

The *w* or the *y* that is vowelled by a ḍamma and preceded by a fatḥa is changed into an *ā.* Thus:

-awu ➠ *-(a)ā*

-ayu ➠ *-(a)ā*

This sequence occurs in the verb with 2nd radical *w* in the perfect formed according to the conjugation *faᶜula,* e.g. *ṭawula* that becomes *ṭ(a)āla* "to become long" and in the verb with 3rd radical *w* or *y* of the conjucation *faᶜala* that occurs in the 3rd person of the masc. pl., e.g. *ġazaw(u)-ū / ġazaw(u)-w* that becomes at first *ġaz(a)ā-w* with this change, then *ġaza-w* "they attacked" with the elision of the *ā,* and *ramay(u)-ū / ramay(u)-w* that becomes at first *ram(a)ā-w* with this change, then *rama-w* "they threw" with the elision of the *ā.*

2.1.4.1. The soundness of the glide:

The glide remains sound in this case:

1- The glide should not be vowelled by a vowel that is not supplied by the basic form.

1- The glide should not be vowelled by a vowel that is not supplied by the basic form:

The *wu* that is preceded by a fatḥa is not changed into an *ā* if the ḍamma of the *w* is not supplied by the basic form (for this condition see Åkesson, *Ibn Masᶜūd* 284: fol. 27b, Bohas/ Kouloughli, *Linguistic* 85), but by an external factor.

This is the case of the verb with 3rd radical *w daᶜawa* "to call" that occurs in the 3rd person of the masc. pl. *daᶜaw* دَعَوا with *alif mamdūda,* followed by a noun to which the *-l* of the definite article following the *waṣla,* is prefixed to, e.g. *da^c aw(u) l-qawma* دَعَوُا ٱلْقَوْمَ "they called for the people" (cf. Åkesson, *Ibn Mas^c ūd* 284: fol. 28a). As remarked the suffixed pronoun of the agent, namely the *w* of the pl. of *da^c aw,* is underlyingly vowelless, but becomes vowelled by the ḍamma that is a vowel of juncture (for discussions concerning the vowel of juncture see Roman, *Étude II,* 747-755), to avoid the cluster of two vowelless segments, namely the vowelless *w* that is the pronoun of the agent of دَعَوْا and the vowelless *l-* following the waṣla of the definite article prefixed to the second word *l-qawma.* As the ḍamma in *da^c aw(u)* is not supplied by the basic form, but is due to an external reason that has to do with the second word following it, the *wu* of *da^c aw(u)* remains sound and is not changed into an *ā.*

2.1.5. The glide, the y, is vowelless and preceded by a ḍamma: its change into a w:

The weak vowelless *y* that is preceded by a ḍamma is usually changed into a w (cf. Åkesson, *Ibn Mas^c ūd* 282: 27a, Wright, II, 80). Thus:

-uy ➠ *-uw > (u)ū*

This sequence occurs in verbs with 1st radical *y* in the imperfect of the passive voice of Form I *yuf^{c}alu,* e.g. *yuysaru* "is pleased" that becomes *yuwsaru* > *y(u)ūsaru,* the active voice of Form IV of the imperfect *yuf^{c}ilu,* e.g. *yuysiru* that becomes *yuwsiru* > *y(u)ūsiru* "is well off" and the active participle of Form IV *muf^{c}ilun,* e.g. *muysirun* that becomes *muwsirun* > *m(u)ūsirun* "is prosperous".

2.1.6. The glide is vowelled by a kasra and preceded by a ḍamma: the transfer of the kasra to the preceding segment and hence the change of the preceding segment's ḍamma into a kasra, the change of the w into a y or the y into an ī respectively, or the elision of the glide's kasra and the lengthening of the ḍamma preceding it into an ū:

The *w* that is vowelled by a kasra and preceded by a ḍamma is considered as unsound and gives hand to two possibilities.

1st possibility: *-uwi* with the *w* vowelled by a kasra and preceded by a ḍamma becomes *-iw* after that the *w's* kasra is shifted before the *w* and hence the ḍamma is changed into a kasra. As in it the vowelless *w* is preceded by a kasra, the *w* is changed into an *ī:* lengthened *ī,* namely *-iy / (i)ī* (cf. Åkesson, *Ibn Mas^{c}ūd* 294: fol. 31b, Bakkūš, *Taṣrīf* 146, ^{c}Abd al-Raḥīm, *Ṣarf* 31-32).

An example of this sequence is found in a verb with 2nd radical *w* in the passive voice formed according to *fu*ᶜ*ila,* e.g. *quwila* "it was said". According to this theory *quwila* > *qiwla* > *q(i)yla* > *q(i)īla* can be mentioned.

2nd possibility: *-uwi* with the *w* vowelled by a kasra and preceded by a ḍamma becomes *–uw* after that the *w's* kasra is elided for the sake of alleviation. As in it the vowelless *w* is preceded by a ḍamma, the *w* is changed into an *ū:* lengthened *ū* so that it becomes *-(u)ū.* According to this theory the example *quwila* > *quwla* > *q(u)ūla* can be mentioned (cf. Åkesson, *Ibn Mas*ᶜ*ūd* 294). This is the dialectal variant of the Banū Asad (for discussions see Bakkūš, *Taṣrīf* 146-147). The changes can be illustrated in this manner:

quwila with the 2nd radical *w* vowelled by a kasra and preceded by ḍamma becomes *quwla* after that the *w's* kasra is elided to alleviate. As the vowelless *w* is preceded by a ḍamma in it, the *w* is lengthened into an *ū,* or in other words the *w* is assimilated to the ḍamma resulting in *q(u)ūla.*

According to another dialectal variant, the ᵓ*išmām,* i.e. "giving the vowel preceding the glide a flavour of the ḍamma so that it notifies of the underlying form", is carried out: *q(i)īla* is said *quila.*

Hence the following variants with the vowelled pronoun of the agent in the perfect can be mentioned (cf. Sībawaihi, II, 398, Ibn Ǧinnī, *Munṣif I,* 293-295, Åkesson, *Ibn Mas*^{c}*ūd* 294: fol. 31b, Howell, IV, fasc. I, 1476-1484):

Form I *quwil-na* with the *-na* ➠ 1- *qil-na* "were said /fem. pl."

➠ 2- *qu(u)ūl-na*

➠ 3- *$^{\circ}$išmām: quil-na*

The *y* that is vowelled by a kasra and preceded by a ḍamma is also considered as unsound. The two possibilities concerning the phonological changes that can be carried out are the following:

1st possibility: *-uyi* with the *y* vowelled by a kasra and preceded by a ḍamma becomes *-iy* after that the *y's* kasra is shifted before the *y* and hence the ḍamma is changed into a kasra. As there is in it a vowelless *y* preceded by a kasra the *y* is changed into an *ī:* lengthened *ī,* so that it becomes *(i)ī.*

An example of this sequence is found in a verb with 2nd radical *y* in the passive voice formed according to *fu*^{c}*ila,* e.g. *buyi*^{c}*a* "it was sold". According to this theory, the changes are the following: *buyi*^{c}*a* > *biy*^{c}*a* > *b(i)ī*^{c}*a.*

2nd possibility: *-uyi* with the *y* vowelled by a kasra and preceded by a ḍamma becomes *-uy* after that the *y's* kasra is elided for the sake of alleviation. As there is in it a vowelless *y* preceded by a ḍamma, the *y* is changed into a *w,* so that it becomes *-uw.* As there is in it a vowelless *w* preceded by a ḍamma, the *w* is changed into an *ū:* lengthened *ū,* so that it becomes *-(u)ū.* According to this theory the example *buyiᶜa* > *buyᶜa* > *b(u)ūᶜa* can be mentioned.

The *ᵓišmām* can also be carried out in it, namely *buiᶜa.*

Hence the following variants with the vowelled pronoun of the agent in the perfect can be mentioned:

Form I *buyiᶜ-na* with the *-na* ➠ 1- *biᶜ-na* "were sold /fem. pl.".

➠ 2- *b(u)ūᶜ-na*

➠ 3- *ᵓišmām: buiᶜ-na*

2.1.7. The glide is vowelled by a ḍamma and preceded by a vowel: the glide's ḍamma is elided:

The glide that is vowelled by a ḍamma and preceded by a vowel is considered as unsound, and the phonological change that is carried out in this sequence results in the elision of the glide's ḍamma to alleviate, because the combination is deemed as heavy.

If the glide is a *w* vowelled by a ḍamma and preceded by one, the procedure is the following: *-uwu* with the *w* vowelled by a ḍamma and preceded by one becomes *-uw* > *-(u)ū* after that the ḍamma is elided and the *w* is changed into an *ū:* lengthened *ū*.

An example of such a sequence is found in the verb in the imperfect of the 3rd person of the masc. sing. *yaġzuwu* "he attacks" that becomes *yaġzuw / yaġz(u)ū*.

If the glide is a *y* vowelled by a ḍamma and preceded by a kasra, the procedure is the following: *-iyu* with the *y* vowelled by a ḍamma and preceded by a kasra that becomes *iy* > *(i)ī* after that the ḍamma is elided and the *y* is changed into an *ī:* lengthened *ī*.

An example of such a sequence is found in the verb in the imperfect of the 3rd person of the masc. sing. *yarmiyu* "he throws" that becomes *yarmiy* > *yarm(i)ī*.

2.1.8. The glide is vowelled by a fatḥa and preceded by a ḍamma: its soundness:

The glide that is vowelled by a fatḥa and preceded by a ḍamma remains sound. The reason of its soundness is the lightness of the fatḥa (cf. Åkesson, *Ibn Mas*ᶜ*ūd* 286: fol. 28b).

-uwa ➠ *-uwa*

-uya ➠ *-uya*

An example in which such a sequence is found is a verb with 3rd radical *w* that occurs in the subjunctive of the 3rd person of the masc. sing., e.g. *lan yad*^{c}*uwa* "he shall not call", in which the 3rd radical *w* of the verb is vowelled by the fatḥa, as a marker of the subjunctive, and is preceded by a ḍamma. This *w* remains sound in spite of the fact that it is preceded by a ḍamma, which could have resulted in the assimilation of the *w* to the ḍamma and thus in the lengthened *w: ū,* i.e. *lan yad*^{c}*(u)ū.* The reason why the phonological change is not carried out in it is that the fatḥa is considered as light on the *w* (for other examples see Ibn Ǧinnī, *Munṣif II,* 114). So there is no need to alleviate more by having *lan yad*^{c}*(u)ū* instead of *lan yad*^{c}*uwa.* We can remark as well that if this was to occur the subjunctive would be mixed up with the jussive.

In line with this theory that the glide vowelled by a fatḥa and preceded by a ḍamma remains sound, the *w* vowelled by a fatḥa and preceded by a ḍamma in *nuwamatun* "one who sleeps much" and the *y* vowelled by a fatḥa and preceded by a ḍamma in ^{c}*uyabatun* "one who reproaches people much" (cf. Zamaḫšarī, 181, Ibn Ya^{c}īš, X, 82-83, Åkesson, *Ibn Mas*^{c}*ūd* 286: fol. 28b) remain sound.

2.1.9. The glide, the w, is vowelled by a fatḥa and preceded by a kasra: its change into a y:

The *w* that is vowelled by a fatḥa and preceded by a kasra is usually changed into a *y*.

-iwa → *-iya*

An example in which such a sequence occurs is the active participle *dā^{c}iwatun* "the one who invites /fem." (cf. Åkesson, *Ibn Mas^{c}ūd* 286: fol. 28b) with the 3rd radical *w* from the verb *da^{c}awa* "to call", which occurs in the fem. sing., and thus with the fatḥa preceding the *tā$^{\supset}$ marbūṭa.* Hence *d(a)ā^{c}iwatun* with the 3rd radical *w* vowelled by a fatḥa and preceded by a kasra becomes *d(a)ā^{c}iyatun* after the change of the *wa* into a *ya.* The reason why the *w* vowelled by a fatḥa is changed in this sequence into a *y* is the influence of the kasra preceding it and the faintness of the nature of the fatḥa.

2.1.9.1. Some anomalous cases:

An anomalous case in which the *w* is changed into a *y* is *siw(a)āṭun* that becomes *siy(a)āṭun* "whips". The phonological change is carried out in it in spite of the fact that it is not formed according to the verbal pattern *fa^{c}al* (for the conditions see 2.1.).

The reason of the unsoundness of the *w(a)* in it is that it is compared to the vowelless *w* of its sing. *sawṭun* (cf. Åkesson, *Ibn Mas*ᶜ*ūd* 284: fol. 28a). Zamaḫšarī, 182 compares the vowelless *w* as well with the vowelless alif of *d(a)ārun* "house". Being then compared with a vowelless segment, the vowelled w in *siw(a)āṭun* is treated as being so, and as it is preceded by a kasra it is changed into the *y*, namely *siy(a)āṭun* (cf. Howell, IV, fasc. I, 1264-1265).

Another example is the broken pl. *diw(a)ārun* with 2nd radical *w* that becomes *diy(a)ārun* (cf. Åkesson, *Ibn Mas*ᶜ*ūd* 284: fol. 28a, Howell, IV, fasc. I, 1264). One of the reasons why the phonological change is carried out in it is so that it is on the analogy of the change that is carried out in its sing. *dawarun* that becomes *d(a)ārun* in which the *wa* is changed into an *ā* because the *w* is vowelled by a fatḥa and preceded by one (cf. Åkesson, *Ibn Mas*ᶜ*ūd 284:* fol. 28a).

Another example is the verbal noun Form I *qiw(a)āmun* that becomes *qiy(a)āmun* "standing". The reason of this change according to Ibn Masᶜūd (Åkesson, *Ibn Mas*ᶜ*ūd* 284: fol. 28a), is that there should be an analogy with the change that is carried out in its verb *qawama* that became *q(a)āma* with the *wa* changed into an *ā*.

2.1.10. The glide, the y, is vowelled by a ḍamma and preceded by a kasra: the transfer of the ḍamma before the y and hence the change of the preceding segment's kasra into a ḍamma, the elision of the y and the lengthening of the ḍamma into an ū according to a theory, or the elision of the y's ḍamma together with the elision of the y and the change of the preceding segment's kasra into a ḍamma according to another theory:

An example in which the *y* is vowelled by a ḍamma and preceded by a kasra is the verb with 3rd weak *y raḍiya* "to be pleased" in the perfect of the 3rd person of the masc. pl. to which the suffix marking the pl., the *ū,* is attached to, namely *raḍiy(u)-ū* "they were pleased /masc. pl." (cf. Åkesson, *Ibn Mas^{c}ūd* 286: fol. 28b).

There are two theories concerning the phonological changes.

The first theory is that *-iy(u)-ū* with the *y* vowelled by a ḍamma and preceded by a kasra becomes *-uy-ū* after that the *y's* ḍamma is shifted backwards, and hence the preceding segment's kasra is changed into a ḍamma. As there is in it a cluster of two vowelless segments, the *y* and *ū,* the *y* is elided so that it becomes *(u)-ū.*

This procedure goes back to Ibn Ǧinnī's theory (cf. Ibn Ǧinnī, *Munṣif II,* 126). An example that he mentions is *raḍiy(u)-ū >raḍuy-ū > raḍ(u)-ū.*

According to Ibn Masᶜūd (cf. Åkesson, *Ibn Masᶜūd* 286: fol. 28b) the phonological changes are the following:

raḍiy(u)-ū> raḍiy-ū > raḍi-ū > raḍ(u)-ū

The second theory is that *-iy(u)-ū* with the *y* vowelled by a ḍamma and preceded by a kasra becomes *iy-ū* after that the *y's* ḍamma is elided for the sake of alleviation. As there is in it a cluster of a vowelless *y* and *ū,* the *y* is elided so that it becomes *i-ū.* As the vowelless *ū* is preceded by a kasra, the kasra is changed into a ḍamma so that it becomes *(u)-ū.*

2.1.11. The glide, the y, is vowelled by a kasra and preceded by a kasra: the elision of the vowel of the y together with the y:

The phonological changes involve the elision of the *y's* kasra and the elision of the *y*. They are illustrated in this manner:

The sequence *iy(i)-ī* that occurs in the 2nd person of the fem. sing. of a verb with the 3rd radical *y* vowelled by a kasra and preceded by one becomes *iy-ī* after that the *y's* kasra is alleviated.

As there is in it a cluster of two vowelless segments: the *y* and the *ī,* the 3rd radical *y* is elided so that it becomes *(i)-ī.*

This sequence occurs in the verb in the imperfect of the 2nd person of the fem. sing. *tarmiy(i)īna* that becomes *tarm(i)-īna* "you throw" The phonological changes are the following: *tarmiy(i)-īna > tarmiy-īna > tarm(i)-īna.*

2.1.12. The glide is vowelled by a fatḥa and preceded by a sukūn: the transfer of the fatḥa to the segment preceding it and the change of the w into an ā:

The phonological changes involve the transfer of the glide's fatḥa to the vowelless segment preceding it and the change of the vowelless *w* or *y* into an *ā* on account of the influence of the fatḥa preceding it.

Thus if the glide is a *w,* the procedure is the following:

- *°wa* (*°* stands for vowelless segment) with the *w* vowelled by a fatḥa and preceded by a sukūn becomes *-aw* after that the *w's* fatḥa is shifted to the vowelless segment preceding it. As in it the *w* is preceded by a fatḥa, the *w* is changed into an *ā* so that it becomes *(a)ā.*

If the glide is a *y,* the procedure is the following: - *°ya* with the *y* vowelled by a fatḥa and preceded by a sukūn becomes *-ay* after that the *y's* fatḥa is shifted to the vowelless segment preceding it.

Some examples in which such a sequence occurs are the verb with 2nd radical *w* formed according to the conjugation *yafᶜalu* that occurs in the imperfect, e.g. *yaḫwafu* that becomes *yaḫawfu* and then *yaḫ(a)āfu* "he is afraid", the imperfect of the passive voice of the verb with 2nd radical *w* or *y* formed according to *yufᶜalu,* e.g. *yuqwalu* that becomes *yuqawlu* and then *yuq(a)ālu* "is said" and *yubyaᶜu* that becomes *yubayᶜu* and then *yub(a)āᶜu* "is sold" and the noun of place of a verb with 2nd radical *w,* e.g. *maqwalun* that becomes *maqawlun* and then *maq(a)ālun* "speech".

2.1.12.1. The soundness of the glide:

The glide remains sound in the noun or in the adjective in the following case that is discussed below, just to mention one:

1- The noun or the adjective is not formed according to the verbal form *faᶜal.*

1- The noun or the adjective is not formed according to the verbal form faᶜal:

An example is the noun *ǧadwalun* "a rivulet" (cf. Åkesson, *Ibn Masᶜūd* 286: fol. 29a, Howell, IV, fasc. I, 1524), in which the *w* is vowelled by a fatḥa and preceded by a sukūn, from *ǧadala* "to make firm".

The reason of the *w's* soundness in it is that the noun is quasi-coordinate to the measure *fa^{c}walun* and hence is not formed according to the verbal *fa^{c}al.* So the *w* could not be changed into an *ā* after that its fatḥa is shifted to the *ǧ* preceding it, i.e. *ǧad(a)ālun,* as this would cancel the formation.

Other examples are *miqwalun* that is contracted from the base form *miqw(a)ālun* "loquacious, eloquent" with 2nd radical *w,* and *miḫyaṭun* that is contracted from the base form *miḫy(a)āṭun* "a needle" (cf. Åkesson, *Ibn Mas^{c}ūd* 288: fol. 29a) with 2nd radical *y.* So their pattern *mif^{c}alun* is the contracted form of *mif^{c}(a)ālun.*

<u>*2.1.12.2. Some anomalous cases:*</u>

An anomalous case that can be taken up, which is due to a sequence of two glides instead of a glide preceded by a consonantal segment, is the verbal noun *kaywan(u)ūnatun* (that is on the pattern *fay^{c}al(u)ūlatun,* cf. Ibn Ǧinnī, *Munṣif II,* 10), in which the 2nd radical *w* is vowelled by a fatḥa and preceded by a vowelless *y.* The phonological changes that are carried out are the change of the *w* into a *y* and the assimilation of the *y* to the *y* resulting in *kayyan(u)ūnatun* "being".

Thus *kaywan(u)ūnatun* with the 2nd radical *w* vowelled by a fatḥa and preceded by a vowelless *y* becomes *kayyan(u)ūnatun* after the change of the *wa* into a *ya* and the assimilation of the yāʾs.

The base form *kayyan(u)ūnatun* is used mostly in poetic licence. It occurs in this verse said by al-Nahšalī, cited by Ibn Ğinnī, *Munṣif II,* 15, Ibn al-Anbārī, *Inṣāf* Q. 115, 334, Suyūṭī, *Ašbāh III,* 335, Ibn Manzūr, V, 3926, Howell, IV, fasc. I, 1461, Åkesson, *Ibn Masᶜūd* 300: (263):

> *"Yā layta ʾannā ḍammanā safīnah*
> *ḥattā yaᶜūda l-waṣlu kayyanūnah".*
> "O would that we and the beloved were so placed
> that a boat held us,
> to the end that union might return in being!".

An alleviated form exists as well, namely *kayn(u)ūnatun* (cf. Åkesson, *Ibn Masᶜūd* 282: fol. 27a-27b) that is from *kayyan(u)ūnatun* after that the 2nd *y* vowelled by a fatḥa is elided.

An analysis of *kayn(u)ūnatun* shows that it occurs with a *y* following the 1st radical, and not with a *w,* - in spite of the fact that it is a verbal noun of a verb with 2nd radical *w* namely *kawana* "to be". The reason of that is that it is made formed according to the verbal nouns of verbs with 2nd radical *y* (cf. ibid 282: fol. 27b, Wright, II, 120) on the basis that they are much more numerous.

Four words of patterns of verbal nouns with *w* as 2nd radical seem to occur formed according to *fay^{c}al(u)ūlatun* (cf. Ibn Manẓūr, V, 3959, Åkesson, *Ibn Mas^{c}ūd* 282-284: fol. 27b): namely:

1- *kayn(u)ūnatun* from *k(a)āna yak(u)ūnu* "to be".

2- *daym(u)ūmatun* from *d(a)āma yad(u)ūmu* "to continue".

3- *sayd(u)ūdatun* from *s(a)āda yas(u)ūdu* "to rule".

4- *hay^{c}(u)ū^{c}atun* from *h(a)ā^{c}a yah(u)ū^{c}u* "to vomit".

Some examples of verbal nouns of verbs with 2nd radical *y* to which *kayn(u)ūnatun* is formed according to, are: *ṣayr(u)ūratun* from *ṣ(a)āra yaṣ(i)īru* "to become", *ġayb(u)ūbatun* from *ġ(a)āba yaġ(i)ību* "to be unconscious" and *qayl(u)ūlatun* from *q(a)āla yaq(i)īlu* "to take a midday nap".

Another anomalous example that can be taken up in which the phonological change is carried out in spite of the fact that two phonological changes due to the unsound glides should be avoided and not combined, is the verbal noun Form IV *ʾiqw(a)āmun* (cf. Åkesson, *Ibn Masʿūd* 288: fols. 29a-29b) that becomes *ʾiq(a)āmatun* "performance". The changes that we observe are the following:

ʾiqw(a)āmun > *ʾiq(a)āāmun* (with the forbidden combination of two vowelless *ā*) > *ʾiq(a)āmun* (with the elision of one *ā)* > *ʾiq(a)āmatun* (with the compensation of the elided *ā* by the suffixed *tāʾ marbūṭa).*

Concerning *ʾiq(a)āāmun* with the combination of the forbidden vowelless glides in this process, it can be mentioned that some grammarians believed that it is the 1st *ā* that is substituted for the 2nd *w* radical vowelled by a fatḥa from *ʾiqw(a)āmun* that is elided, whereas others believed that it is the 2nd one which is the infixed *ā* of *ʾifʿ(a)ālatun* (cf. Ibn Yaʿīš, VI, 58). About it and its likes, Ibn Ǧinnī, *Munṣif I,* 291-292 remarks:

> "The original forms of *ʾiq(a)āmatun* "erecting", *ʾiḫ(a)āfatun* "frightening" and *ʾib(a)ānatun* "explanation" are: *ʾiqw(a)āmatun,* *ʾiḫw(a)āfatun* and *ʾiby(a)ānatun.* They intended to carry out a phonological change due to the unsoundness of the glide in the *maṣdar* that is in conformity with the phonological change that is carried out in

[their verbs] *ʾaq(a)āma* "to erect" and *ʾab(a)āna* "to explain". So they shifted the fatḥa from the *w* [of *ʾiqw(a)āmatun]* and from the *y* [of *ʾiby(a)ānatun]* to the segment preceding them [i.e. *ʾiqawāmatun* and *ʾibayānatun],* then they changed them [i.e. the *w* and the *y* respectively] into an *ā* preceding the infixed *ā* of *ʾifᶜ(a)ālatun,* so they became as you remark *ʾiq(a)āāmatun* and *ʾib(a)āānatun.* Abū l-Ḥasan believed that the elided *ā* is the 1st *ā* whereas al-Ḫalīl believed that it is the 2nd one, which is the infixed one, according to what has been presented among both their teachings".

2.1.13. The glide, the y, is vowelled by a kasra and preceded by a sukūn: the transfer of the kasra to the segment preceding it and the change of the y into an ī:

The phonological changes involve the transfer of the *y's* kasra to the vowelless segment preceding it and the change of the *y* into an *ī*. Thus:

- °*yi* ➠ -*iy*

(° stands for vowelless segment)

An example in which such a sequence occurs is the verb with 2nd radical *y* that is formed according to the conjugation *yaf^{c}ilu* in the imperfect, e.g. *yabyi^{c}u* > *yabiy^{c}u* > *yab(i)ī^{c}u* "he sells".

2.1.13.1. Anomalous cases:

An anomalous case due to a sequence of two glides following each other instead of a glide preceded by a consonantal segment, is *mawyitun* "a dead man", in which the *y* vowelled by a kasra is preceded by the vowelless 2nd radical *w*. The result is the change of the *w* into a *y* and the assimilation of the *y* to the *y*.

Thus *mawyitun* with the *y* vowelled by a kasra and preceded by a vowelless *w* becomes *mayyitun* after that the *w* is changed into a *y* and the yāʾs are assimilated.

An alleviated form exists as well, namely *maytun* (cf. Åkesson, *Ibn Mas^{c}ūd* 282: fol. 27b) from *mayyitun* in which the 2nd *y* vowelled by a kasra is elided. It occurs in this verse said by an unknown poet, cited by Carter, *Linguistics* [Širbīnī, *Āğurrūmīya]* 376, Åkesson, *Ibn Mas^{c}ūd* 301: (263):

> "*ʾInnamā l-maytu man ya^{c}īšu kaʾīban*
> *kāsifan bāluhu qalīla l-rağāʾi*".
> "The dead man is simply he who lives
> grieving,
> wretched his plight and small of hope".

Both variants *maytun* and *mayyitun* are combined in this verse said by ᶜAdī b. al-Raᶜlā, cited by Muʾaddib, *Taṣrīf* 113, 268, Ibn Yaᶜīš, X, 69, *Mulūkī* 466, Ibn Manẓūr, VI, 4295, Howell, IV, fasc. I, 1461, Åkesson, *Ibn Masᶜūd* 301: (264):

"Laysa man māta fa-starāḥa bi-maytin
ʾinnamā l-maytu mayyitu l-ʾaḥyāʾi".
"He who has died, and taken his rest, is not
really dead:
the really dead is only the dead of the living,
[i.e. is only he that is living, while his state is
like that of the dead]".

2.1.14. The glide is vowelled by a kasra and preceded by a vowelless ā: the change of the wi or yi into ʾi:

Such a sequence occurs in the cases of active participles of verbs with 2nd radical *w* and *y* that are formed according to *f(a)āᶜilun,* in which the *w* or *y* is vowelled by a kasra and preceded by the vowelless *ā*.

The phonological change implies the change of the *wi* or the *yi* into *ʾi.*

The sequence - *āwi* with the *w* vowelled by a kasra and preceded by an *ā* that becomes *-āʾi* after that the *wi* is changed into *ʾi,* can be taken up at first.

An example is *q(a)āwilun* > *q(a)āʾilun* "a sayer" (cf. ʿAbd al-Raḥīm, *Ṣarf* 80):

The sequence *-āyi* with the *y* vowelled by a kasra and preceded by an *ā* that becomes *-āʾi* after that the *yi* is changed into *ʾi*.

An example is *b(a)āyiun* > *b(a)āʾiʿun* "a seller".

2.1.15. The glide, the w, is vowelled by a ḍamma and preceded by a sukūn: the transfer of the ḍamma to the segment preceding it and the change of the w into ū:

The phonological changes concerning this sequence are the following: *-^{o}wu* (^{o} stands for vowelless segment) with the *w* vowelled by a ḍamma and preceded by a sukūn becomes *-uw* after that the *w's* ḍamma is shifted to the vowelless segment preceding it. As the ḍamma precedes the *w*, the *w* is changed into an *ū* or lengthened *u: ū*, so that it becomes *(u)ū.*

Such a sequence is found in the verb with 2nd radical *w* of the conjugation *yafʿulu* that occurs in the imperfect, e.g. *yaqwulu* "he says" > *yaquwlu* > *yaq(u)ūlu,* in the imperative, e.g. *ʾuqwul* "say!" > *ʾuquwl* > *uq(u)ūl,* and then after the elision of the connective hamza and the *ū* > *qul,* and in the passive participle *maqwuwlun* > *maqw(u)ūlun* "what is said" > *maq(u)ūlun.*

2.1.15.1. The soundness of the glide:

The glide remains sound in the noun or in the adjective in the following case:

1- The glide should not be vowelled by a vowel that is not supplied by the basic form.

1- The glide should not be vowelled by a vowel that is not supplied by the basic form:

The *w* remains sound if it is the 3rd radical of a noun that carries the marker of the declension, and thus its vowel is not supplied by the basic form but by an external reason having to do with syntax (for this condition see 2.1. and compare the case of *al-ramyu* "the throwing" that ends with the 3rd radical *y,* see par. 2.1.16.1.: 1). An example is *al-dalwu* "the bucket" with the 3rd radical sound *w.*

2.1.16. The glide, the y, is vowelled by a ḍamma and preceded by a sukūn: the transfer of the ḍamma to the vowelless segment preceding it, the change of the ḍamma into a kasra and the change of the y into ī:

The phonological changes concerning this sequence are the following: *-^{o}yu* (^{o} stands for vowelless segment) with the *y* vowelled by a ḍamma and preceded by a sukūn becomes *-uy* after that the *y's* ḍamma is shifted to the vowelless segment preceding it. As the ḍamma precedes the vowelless *y*, the ḍamma is changed into a kasra so that it becomes *iy*. As the kasra precedes the *y*, the *y* is changed into *ī* or lengthened *i: ī*, so that it becomes *(i)ī*.

Such a sequence occurs in the passive participle of the verb with 2nd radical *y* of the conjugation *yaf^{c}ilu*, e.g. *yabyi^{c}u* "he sells", namely *maby(u)ū^{c}un* "sold" which becomes *mab(i)ī^{c}un*. The steps are *maby(u)ū^{c}un* > *mabuyū^{c}un* of which the *ū* is elided to hinder the succession of two vowelless segments resulting in *mabuy^{c}un* of which the *u* is changed into *i*, namely *mabiy^{c}un* > *mab(i)ī^{c}un* of which the *i* is lengthenened.

2.1.16.1. The soundness of the glide:

The glide remains sound in the noun or in the adjective in the following case:

1- The glide should not be vowelled by a vowel that is not supplied by the basic form.

1- The glide should not be vowelled by a vowel that is not supplied by the basic form:

The *y* remains sound if it is the 3rd radical of a noun that carries the marker of the declension, and thus the vowel is not supplied by the basic form but by an external reason having to do with syntax (for this condition see 2.1. and compare the case of *al-dalwu* with the 3rd radical *w* par. 2.1.15: 2.).

An example is *al-ramyu* "the throwing" (cf. Åkesson, *Ibn Masᶜūd* 286: fol. 29a) in which the *y* is vowelled and preceded by a sukūn. If a phonological change is to be carried out in it, it would imply the transfer of its various vowels of declension: the ḍamma in the case of the nominative, the fatḥa in the case of the accusative and the kasra in the case of the genitive to the vowelless segment preceding this vowel.

In the case of the ḍamma, *al-ramyu* would become *al-ramuy* and then the *y* would have to be changed into a vowelless *w* to accord with the ḍamma preceding it, namely *al-ram(u)ū.*

In the case of the fatḥa, *al-ramya* would become *al-ramay* and then the *y* would have to be changed into a vowelless *ā* to accord with the fatḥa preceding it, namely *al-ram(a)ā.*

In the case of the kasra, *al-ramyi* would become *al-ramiy* and the vowelless *y* would be changed into *ī,* namely *al-ram(i)ī.* In all the three cases, the declinable noun would have to end with a vowelless segment without any marker of declension, which is the reason why it is preferred that in order to safeguard the marker of the declension, the *y,* remains sound.

Another example of a declinable substantive is *al-ẓabyu* "the gazelle" with the 3rd radical sound *y.*

2.1.17. The glide, the w or y, is vowelless and preceded by a kasra: its change into a y or ī respectively:

The general rule is that the vowelless glide that is preceded by a vowel is changed into a segment of the nature of the vowel preceding it. The reason of this change is the weakness of the state of the glide, which is vowelless, and the influence of the vowel, whether it is a kasra or a ḍamma, preceding it, on it (cf. Åkesson, *Ibn Masᶜūd* 282: 27a).

If the glide is a vowelless *w* preceded by a kasra it is changed into a lengthened *y:*

-iw ➠ *-iy > (i)ī*

An example is *miwzānun* that becomes *m(i)yzānun > m(i)īzānun* "balance".

If the glide is a vowelless y preceded by a kasra it is changed into a lengthened *y* (cf. Wright, II, 80).

-iy ➠ *-(i)ī*

An example is the imperative *ᵓiysir* that becomes *ᵓ(i)īsir* "be well off!".

2.1.18. The transposition of segments in some nouns:

An example is *qisiyyun* underlyingly *quw(u)ūsun* which is the pl. of *qawsun* "bow" (cf. Åkesson, *Ibn Masᶜūd* 292: fols. 30b-31a, Howell, I, fasc. III, 930, IV, fasc. I, 1583-1585, de Sacy, I, 108, Vernier, I, 340-341). It can be remarked that *quw(u)ūsun* is formed according to the pattern *fuᶜ(u)ūlun* in which the radicals are transposed resulting in *qusuwwun* formed according to *ful(u)ūᶜun* and not *fuᶜ(u)ūlun,* as if it is the pl. of *qaswun* and not of *qawsun.* In *qusuwwun* the wāws are changed into yāᵓs because they occur at the extremity of the word, which is deemed as heavy, resulting in *qusuyyun,* then the ḍamma of the *s* is changed into a kasra because of the *y's* influence, resulting in *qusiyyun.* The *q* becomes then vowelled with a kasra on the analogy of the kasra and of the *y* following it, so that it became *qisiyyun.* The same phenomenon occurs with *ᶜiṣiyyun* or *ᶜuṣiyyun* pl. of *ᶜaṣā* "stick" (cf. ibid).

Another example in which the transposition of segments occurs is the pl. of *n(a)āqatun* namely *ᵓanwuqun.* As the ḍamma is deemed heavy upon the *w,* the *w* is transposed made to precede the *n* resulting in *ᵓawnuqun,* then the *y* is substituted for the *w* resulting in *ᵓaynuqun* (cf. Åkesson, *Ibn Masᶜūd* 292: fol. 31a, Howell, I, fasc. III, 1074). This change of the *w* into a *y* does not follow the analogy as the *w* is vowelless and is preceded by fatḥa, but it is carried out for the sake of alleviation.

3. BIBLIOGRAPHY

3.1. Primary sources

ᶜAbd al-Raḥīm, Ṣarf = ᶜAbd al-Raḥīm, Saᶜd, Muqaddamat fī ᶜilm al-ṣarf, Cairo s.a.

Åkesson, *Ibn Masᶜūd* = Åkesson, J. , *Arabic Morphology and Phonology based on the Marāḥ al-arwāḥ by Aḥmad b. ᶜAlī b. Masᶜūd, Presented with an Introduction, Arabic Edition, English Translation and Commentary,* Leiden 2001.

Bakkūš, *Taṣrif* = Al-Bakkūš, Ṭ., *al-Taṣrif al-ᶜarabī,* Tunis 1973.

Carter, *Linguistics [Širbīnī, Āğurrūmīya]* = Carter, M. G., *Arab Linguistics, an introductory classical text with translation and notes,* Amsterdam 1981.

Ibn al-Anbārī, *Inṣāf* = Ibn al-Anbārī, Abū l-Barakāt, *Kitāb al-inṣāf fī masāʾil al-ḫilāf bayna l-naḥwīyīn al-baṣrīyīn wa-l-kūfīyīn: Die grammatischen Schulen von Kufa und Basra,* Ed. G. Weil, Leiden 1913.

Ibn Ğinnī, *de Flexione* = Ibn Ğinnîi, Abū l-Fatḥ ᶜUṯmān, *de Flexione Libellvs,* Ed. G. Hoberg, Lipsiae, 1885.

Ibn Ğinnī, *Ḫaṣāʾiṣ* = Ibn Ğinnī, Abū l-Fatḥ ᶜUṯmān, *al-Ḫaṣāʾiṣ,* Ed. M. A. al-Naǧǧār, 3 vol., Cairo 1371/1952-1376/1956.

Ibn Ğinnī, *Munṣif* = Ibn Ğinnī, Abū l-Fatḥ ᶜUṯmān, *al-Munṣif fī šarḥ taṣrīf al-Māzinī,* Ed. I. Muṣṭafā, ᶜA. Amīn, 3 vol., Cairo 1373/1954-1379/1960.

Ibn Ğinnī, *Sirr* = Ibn Ğinnī, Abū l-Fatḥ ᶜUṯmān, *Sirr ṣināᶜat al-iᶜrāb,* Ed. Ḥ. Hindāwī, 2 vol., Damascus 1405/1985.

Ibn Ḫālawaihi, *Qirāʾāt* = Ibn Ḫālawaihi, Abū ᶜAbd Allāh al-Ḥusain b. Aḥmad, *Iᶜrāb al-qirāʾāt al-sabᶜ wa-ᶜilaluhā,* Ed. ᶜAbd al-Raḥmān b. Sulaimān al-ᶜAtīmain, 2 vol., Cairo 1413/1992.

Ibn Manẓūr = Ibn Manẓūr, Ǧamāl al-Dīn, *Lisān al-ᶜArab,* 6 vol., Beirut undated.

Ibn al-Sarrāǧ, *ᵓUṣūl* = Ibn al-Sarrāǧ, Abū Bakr, *al-ᵓUṣūl fī l-Naḥw,* Ed. ᶜA. Ḥ. al-Fatlī, Beirut 1408/1988.

Ibn ᶜUṣfūr = Ibn ᶜUṣfūr al-Ašbīlī, Abū l-ᶜAbbās ᶜAlī b. Muᵓmin, *al-Mumtiᶜ fī l-taṣrīf,* Ed. F. al-Dīn Qabāwih, Aleppo 1390/1970.

Ibn Wallād, *Maqṣūr* = Ibn Wallād, Abū l-ᶜAbbās Aḥmad b. Muḥammad, *Kitāb al-maqṣūr wa-l-mamdūd ᶜalā ḥurūf al-muᶜǧam,* Part I, Contributions towards Arabic Philology, Ed. Paul Brönnle, Leiden 1900.

Ibn Yaᶜīš = Ibn Yaᶜīš, Muwaffaq al-Dīn Abū l-Barāᵓ Yaᶜīš, *Šarḥ al-mufaṣṣal, 2* vol., Beirut undated.

Ibn Yaᶜīš, *Mulūkī* = Ibn Yaᶜīš, Muwaffaq al-Dīn Abū l-Barāᵓ Yaᶜīš, *Šarḥ al-mulūkī fī l-taṣrīf,* Ed. Faḫr al-Dīn Qabāwa, Aleppo 1393/1973.

Muᵓaddib, *Taṣrīf* = Al-Muᵓaddib, al-Qāsim b. Muḥammad b. Saᶜīd, *Daqāᵓiq al-taṣrīf,* Ed. A. N. al-Qaisī, Ḥ. Ṣ. al-Ḍāmin and Ḥ. Tūrāl, Iraq 1407/1987.

Sībawaihi = Sîbawaihi, Abū Bišr ᶜAmr b. ᶜUṯmān, *Le Livre de Sîbawaihi (Kitāb Sībawaihi), Traité de grammaire arabe,*

Ed. H. Derenbourg, 2 vol., Paris 1881-1889. Réimpression: 1970.

Širbīnī, *Āğurrūmīya* = see Carter, *Linguistics.*

Suyūṭī, *Ašbāh* = Al-Suyūtī, Ğalāl al-Dīn Abū l-Faḍl ᶜAbd al-Raḥmān, *al-ᵓAšbāh wa-l-naẓāᵓir,* Ed. ᶜAbd AIlāh Nabhān, 4 vol., Damascus 1406/1985.

Suyūṭī, *Muzhir* = Al-Suyūtī, Ğalāl al-Dīn Abū l-Faḍl ᶜAbd al-Raḥmān, *al-Muzhir fī ᶜulūm al-luġa wa-anwāᶜihā,* 2 vol., Cairo s.a.

Zamaḫšarī = Zamaḫsᵓario, Abū l-Qāsim Maḥmūd b. ᶜUmar, *al-Mufaṣṣal,* Ed. J. P. Broch, Christianiae 1840.

3.2. Secondary sources

Åkesson, *Conversion* = Åkesson, J., *Conversion of the yāᵓ into an alif in Classical Arabic* in: ZAL 31, Wiesbaden 1996.

Åkesson, *Ibn Masᶜūd* = Åkesson, J., *Arabic Morphology and Phonology based on the Marāḥ al-arwāḥ by Aḥmad b. ᶜAlī b. Masᶜūd, Presented with an Introduction, Arabic Edition, English Translation and Commentary,* Leiden 2001.

Bohas/Kouloughli, Linguistic = Bohas, G., Guillaume, J.-P., Kouloughli, D.E., The Arabic Linguistic Tradition, London and New York 1990.

Carter, *Linguistics* [Širbīnī, *Āğurrūmīya]* = Carter, M. G., *Arab Linguistics, an introductory classical text with translation and notes,* Amsterdam 1981.

Fleisch, *Traité I* = Fleisch, H., *Traité de Philologie Arabe, vol. I, Préliminaires, Phonétique Morphologie Nominale,* Beyrouth 1961.

Fleisch, *Traité II* = Fleisch, H., *Traité de Philologie Arabe, vol. II, Pronoms, Morphologie verbale, Particules,* Beyrouth 1979.

Howell = Howell, M. S., *Grammar of the Classical Arabic Language,* 4 parts in 7 vol., Allahabad 1880-1911.

Lane = Lane, E.W., *Arabic-English Lexicon,* 8 in 2 vol., London 1863-1893. Reprint: 1984.

Monteil, *Abū Nuwās* = Abû Nuwâs, *Le vin, le vent, la vie,* Introduction critique et choix de poèmes traduits de l'arabe par Vincent Monteil, Calligraphies de Hassan Massoudy, 2nde édition, Paris 1979.

Nöldeke, *Grammatik* = Nöldeke, T., *Zur Grammatik des Classischen Arabisch im Anhang: Die Handschriftlichen ergänzungen in dem Handexemplar Theodor Nöldekes bearbeitet und mit zuzätzen versehen von Anton Spitaler,* Darmstadt 1963.

Rāğiḥī, *Basīṭ* = Rāğiḥī, ᶜAbdo, *al-Basīṭ fī ᶜilm al-ṣarf,* Alexandria s.a.

Roman, *Étude* = Roman, A., *Étude de la phonologie et de la morphologie de la koinè arabe,* 2 vol., Publications de l'Université de Provence, Marseille 1983.

De Sacy = De Sacy, S., *Grammaire arabe,* 2 vol., Tunis 1904-1905.

Talmon, *ᶜAyn* = Talmon, R., *Arabic Grammar in its formative Age, Kitāb al-ᶜAyn and its Attribution to Ḫalīl b. Aḥmad,* Leiden - New York - Køln 1997.

Vernier = Vernier, D., *Grammaire arabe,* 2 vol., Beyrouth 1891.

Wright = Wright, W., *A Grammar of the Arabic Language,* Cambridge, Third Edition 1985.

Wright, *Comparative Grammar* = Wright, W., *Lectures on the Comparative Grammar of the Semitic Languages,* Cambridge 1890.

4. INDEX OF QUR'ANIC QUOTATIONS

5. INDEX OF VERSES

6. INDEX OF NAMES

www.ingramcontent.com/pod-product-compliance
Lightning Source LLC
Chambersburg PA
CBHW021011090426
42738CB00007B/741
* 9 7 8 9 1 9 7 7 6 4 1 9 3 *